CHRIS BUSH

Chris Bush is a Sheffield-born playwright, lyricist and theatre-maker. Past work includes *The Changing Room* (National Theatre Connections); *A Declaration from the People* (Dorfman, National Theatre); *What We Wished For*, *A Dream*, *The Sheffield Mysteries*, *20 Tiny Plays about Sheffield* (Sheffield Theatres); *Transcending* (Orange Tree Theatre); *Larksong* (New Vic Theatre); *Cards on the Table* (Royal Exchange Theatre); *ODD* (Royal & Derngate, Northampton: concert performance); *Sleight & Hand* (Summerhall/Odeon Cinemas/BBC Arts); *TONY! The Blair Musical* (York Theatre Royal/tour); *Speaking Freely*, *Poking the Bear* (Theatre503); *The Bureau of Lost Things* (Theatre503/Rose Bruford) and *Wolf* (Latitude Festival). Forthcoming work in 2018 includes *Pericles* (Olivier, National Theatre) and *Steel* (Sheffield Theatres). Chris has won the National Young Playwrights' Festival, a Brit Writers' Award and the Perfect Pitch Award. She has previously been Playwright in Residence for Sheffield Theatres, and part of writers' groups at the National Theatre, Orange Tree and Royal Exchange, Manchester.

MATT WINKWORTH

Matt Winkworth is an Oxford-born composer. He was artist-in-residence at the Oxford Playhouse 2016–17 and with Chris Bush won the Perfect Pitch Award in 2014. Recent credits include *SOLE* (OFS, Oxford); *Elves and the Shoemaker* (Jacquline du Pré, Oxford); *High as Sugar* (Brighton Fringe, King's Head Theatre, OFS); *Death and Chocolate* (Lost Theatre); *Attempts On Her Life*, *Under Milk Wood*, *Animal Farm* (Oxford Playhouse Young Company); *The Bureau of Lost Things* (Theatre503); *ODD* (Perfect Pitch/Royal & Derngate Northampton: concert performance).

Other Titles in this Series

Mike Bartlett
ALBION
BULL
GAME
AN INTERVENTION
KING CHARLES III
WILD

Tom Basden
THE CROCODILE
HOLES
JOSEPH K
THERE IS A WAR

Jez Butterworth
THE FERRYMAN
JERUSALEM
JEZ BUTTERWORTH PLAYS: ONE
MOJO
THE NIGHT HERON
PARLOUR SONG
THE RIVER
THE WINTERLING

Elinor Cook
THE GIRL'S GUIDE TO SAVING
    THE WORLD
IMAGE OF AN UNKNOWN YOUNG
    WOMAN
THE LADY FROM THE SEA
    after Ibsen
PILGRIMS

Samantha Ellis
CLING TO ME LIKE IVY
HOW TO DATE A FEMINIST

Vivienne Franzmann
BODIES
MOGADISHU
PESTS
THE WITNESS

James Fritz
COMMENT IS FREE &
    START SWIMMING
THE FALL
PARLIAMENT SQUARE
ROSS & RACHEL

Stacey Gregg
LAGAN
OVERRIDE
PERVE
SCORCH
SHIBBOLETH
WHEN COWS GO BOOM

Alan Harris
HOW MY LIGHT IS SPENT
LOVE, LIES AND TAXIDERMY
SUGAR BABY

Sam Holcroft
COCKROACH
DANCING BEARS
EDGAR & ANNABEL
PINK
RULES FOR LIVING
THE WARDROBE
WHILE YOU LIE

Vicky Jones
THE ONE
TOUCH

Anna Jordan
CHICKEN SHOP
FREAK
YEN

Lucy Kirkwood
BEAUTY AND THE BEAST
    with Katie Mitchell
BLOODY WIMMIN
THE CHILDREN
CHIMERICA
HEDDA *after* Ibsen
IT FELT EMPTY WHEN THE
    HEART WENT AT FIRST BUT
    IT IS ALRIGHT NOW
LUCY KIRKWOOD PLAYS: ONE
MOSQUITOES
NSFW
TINDERBOX

Evan Placey
CONSENSUAL
GIRLS LIKE THAT
GIRLS LIKE THAT & OTHER PLAYS
    FOR TEENAGERS
JEKYLL & HYDE *after* R.L. Stevenson
PRONOUN

Jack Thorne
2ND MAY 1997
BUNNY
BURYING YOUR BROTHER IN
    THE PAVEMENT
A CHRISTMAS CAROL *after* Dickens
HOPE
JACK THORNE PLAYS: ONE
JUNKYARD
LET THE RIGHT ONE IN
    after John Ajvide Lindqvist
MYDIDAE
THE SOLID LIFE OF SUGAR WATER
STACY & FANNY AND FAGGOT
WHEN YOU CURE ME
WOYZECK *after* Büchner

Phoebe Waller-Bridge
FLEABAG

Chris Bush

THE ASSASSINATION OF KATIE HOPKINS

Music by
Matt Winkworth

NICK HERN BOOKS
London
www.nickhernbooks.co.uk

A Nick Hern Book

The Assassination of Katie Hopkins first published in Great Britain as a paperback original in 2018 by Nick Hern Books Limited, The Glasshouse, 49a Goldhawk Road, London W12 8QP

The Assassination of Katie Hopkins copyright © 2018 Chris Bush

Chris Bush has asserted her right to be identified as the author of this work

Cover design: SWD

Designed and typeset by Nick Hern Books, London
Printed in Great Britain by Mimeo Ltd, Huntingdon, Cambridgeshire PE29 6XX

A CIP catalogue record for this book is available from the British Library

ISBN 978 1 84842 760 0

The Assassination of Katie Hopkins was first performed at
Theatr Clwyd, Mold, on 20 April 2018, with the following cast:

AMY BOOTH-STEEL
RAKESH BOURY
CHÉ FRANCIS
DEREK HUTCHINSON
GENESIS LYNEA
MAIMUNA MEMON
BETHZIENNA WILLIAMS
MATTHEW WOODYATT

THE BAND

Keyboard One	Jordan Li-Smith
Keyboard Two	Stuart Calvert
Malletkat/Percussion	Tom Daley
Bass	Nathan Welch

Director	James Grieve
Designer	Lucy Osborne
Musical Supervisor	David White
Orchestrator	David White
Movement Director	Lucy Hind
Musical Director	Jordan Li-Smith
Lighting Designer	Oliver Fenwick
Sound Designer	Dominic Kennedy
Video/Projection Designer	Nina Dunn
Assistant Director	Hannah Noone
Assistant Musical Director	Stuart Calvert
Copyist	Stuart Calvert
Keyboard Programmer	Ben Ferguson
Video Engineer/Programmer	Harrison Cooke
Band Fixer	Andy Barnwell
Production Manager	Hannah Lobb
Wardrobe Supervisor	Deborah Knight
Casting	Will Burton

Company Stage Manager	Stevie Haighton
Deputy Stage Manager	Harriet Stewart
Assistant Stage Manager	Linnea Fridén Grønning

Acknowledgements

We're very lucky to have assembled such an amazing team to bring this piece to life. A big thanks to James Grieve, our phenomenal cast, and everyone else involved. Theatr Clwyd isn't just a building, it's a community, and everybody here has constantly gone above and beyond to make us feel welcome (and readily abandoned their day jobs to assemble 2,332 fake mobile-phone units). In particular we're massively indebted to Tamara Harvey, who has been with us on this project since day one, and whose bravery and passion made it possible.

Additional thanks to the National Theatre Studio for cheeky use of rehearsal rooms, Louise Chantal, Jo Noble and Hannah Groombridge at the Oxford Playhouse, Amy Bradbury at Harbottle Lewis, Julia Mills at Berlin Associates, Eddie Gower at Mountview, David Marsland, Steve Winter, Charlie Westenra, Rosie Robinson, Kate Morley, and every actor who did a workshop or reading with us: Natalie Dew, Natasha Cottrail, Amanda Wilkin, Verity Quade, Matt Harrop, Alan Vicary, Enyi Okoronkwo, Nic Lamont, Adam Rhys-Davies, Will Bridges, Fiona Drummond, Seyi Omooba, Kevin McMonagie, Ciaran Stewart, Erin Doherty, Lynn Hunter, Bethan Cullinane, Gaby French, Kerry Peers, Edd Campbell Bird, Charlotte Miranda-Smith, Rachel-Mae Brady, Kevin Tomlinson, Abi Hood, Hope McNamara, Jake Morter, Paul Chesterton, Alice Guile, Helen Winter, Krage Brown, Michael Gerard, Anna-Marie Acevedo, Rhiannon Bodman, Hebba Rose Brown, Regan Burke, Imogen Byron, Molly Ellingham, Sally Fellows, Andrew Fanklin, Elizabeth Frisby, Nathan James, Myles Osbourne-Banton, Heather Porte, Alice Schofield, Rosie Skuse, Holly Slater, Rebecca Swindells.

Finally, thank you to our families for their constant support and encouragement. We'll try to upset fewer people with the next show.

Chris Bush and Matt Winkworth,
April 2018

Characters

OWEN	EWAN	CATALINA
SHAYMA	GAVIN	
KAYLEIGH		FAZIL
PAM	PRIME MINISTER	
RICHARD		GRACE
BRIAN	ELENA	JOEY
NINA	SECRETARY	MARK
KARL	DEBBIE	
		RYAN
BENEDICT	DWIGHT	
	FRANKIE	DOMINIC
REBEKAH	MAX	
DAVID	ISSY	MAN 1
CAROL		MAN 2
WESLEY	HARRIS	WOMAN
	DELANEY	
BRANDON		STUART
	DIPO	TERRY
ADAM	MARYAM	PIPPA
TRACEY	FAHAD	OLLIE
DONNA		

Plus various NEWS REPORTERS, ANCHORS, CORRESPONDENTS, JOURNALISTS, TWEETS, STATUS UPDATES, BLOGGERS, PROTESTERS *and other single-line voices to be drawn from the company as needed.*

Notes on text and production

While the events of the play are pure fiction, they are presented as if gathered in a verbatim fashion. Rather than rely solely on interviews and audience address, a lot of the material has a 'found footage' feel; scenes consisting of clips from television or radio broadcasts, YouTube videos, news bulletins, vlogs, minutes from meetings, voicemail messages, etc. – any scenario where real-world events may have plausibly been recorded. Wherever possible we should be seeing this 'original' footage played/projected/incorporated in some way while simultaneously watching its reenactment on stage.

All bold text is sung.

A forward slash (/) indicates an overlap in dialogue where the next character starts speaking.

When the # symbol appears in dialogue, the word 'hashtag' is spoken/sung.

Line breaks are there for ease of reading – they can be ignored wherever not helpful.

This text went to press before the end of rehearsals and so may differ slightly from the play as performed.

ACT ONE

1. Overture: Have You Seen This?

The stage is bare, except for a number of mobile phones on various tables and surfaces. One by one they start to buzz, slowly building a percussive rhythm. Now they begin to bleep and chirp. Gradually, members of the COMPANY *enter. Now the noise of their key tones as they write messages are incorporated into the score, along with the whooshes and chimes as these messages are sent and received. Only now do they start to sing, their voices overlapping.*

COMPANY. **Have you seen this?**
  Have you seen this?
  Have you seen this?
  Have you seen this?

  Have you seen this?
  Fake – totally fake.
  Have you seen this?
  Don't believe a word of it

  Have you seen this?
  Shit – what's going on?
  Have you seen this?
  Read this thread by @SuzieCupcake96

  Have you seen this?
  Shots fired –
  Have you seen this?

A search result is heard.

TWEET. **Fire sweeps through agricultural site near Dartford**

The story is minimised as the COMPANY *keeps searching.*

COMPANY. **Have you seen this?**
  Shots fired in central London

Another search result.

MAN. **Fired up for tonight's sesh in London town – bring on the shots! #ladsontour**

Again, it's closed.

COMPANY. **Have you seen this?**
Shots fired!
Witnesses report a shooting in London
Shots fired!
Shooting London

A CELEBRITY *emerges from the* COMPANY, *sending a tweet and taking a selfie.*

CELEBRITY. **Great to be back shooting in London – one of my all-time favourite cities.**

COMPANY. **Gunshots. Shots fired. Shooting.**
Have you seen this?
Gunshots fired in central London

WOMAN. **Who's letting off fireworks in June? #wankers**

ALL. **#wankers!**

COMPANY. **Gunshots in Mayfair**
Swear to God that sounded just like gunshots in Mayfair

TWEET. We'll be live-streaming from the British Media and Entertainment Awards tonight in Mayfair. #BMEAwards

COMPANY. **Have you seen this?**
Shots fired at the #BMEAwards
Have you seen this?
Ambulances arriving at the #BMEAwards

A series of more official tweets.

TWEET. **Delays on the Jubilee line caused by an incident in Mayfair**

TWEET. **Grosvenor Street is closed due to an incident in Mayfair**

TWEET. **Adjust your travel plans to avoid an incident in Mayfair**

COMPANY. **Shit's going down in Mayfair**
All kicking off in Mayfair
What's going on in Mayfair?

From out of the COMPANY *come three* NEWS
REPORTERS. *The speech is now more formal, clipped,
official. Underscore continues underneath.* NEWS. 1 *and* 2
are in the studio, NEWS. 3 *on the ground, unexpectedly
caught up in the action, trying to hold it together.*

NEWS. 1. We are receiving breaking news of an incident –
Of a suspected shooting –
In the West End of London.
Eyewitnesses / are reporting –

NEWS. 2. If you're just joining us, what we currently –
We believe –
At the moment we believe –
We think an attack / may have occurred –

NEWS. 3. You're joining me, uh, I'm here
At the British Media and Entertainment Awards,
Where there, there / seems to have been –

NEWS. 1. Four ambulances / were seen arriving –

NEWS. 2. Four – we're saying four –

NEWS. 1. At the exclusive Mayfair venue
But it's unclear at this point / just how many –

NEWS. 3. Um, some kind of, of, I think gunfire –

COMPANY. **Have you seen this?**
Bloodbath at the #BMEAwards
Have you seen this?
Terror attack at the #BMEAwards

NEWS. 3. You can see where police have…
They've cordoned off the whole…
The whole… as you can see…
I'm sorry, John. I'm sorry, / this is –

NEWS. 2. Many of us here of course
Have friends – have friends and colleagues
In attendance at the… / present at the –

NEWS. 1. We don't yet have any details of...
    All we know is that there has been an incident
    And we'll keep you updated / on all of the –

NEWS. 3. I see Cathy! I see Cathy from our –
    Lots of... of very, um, of very shaken up, and...
    Understandably. A lot of shock. A lot of...
    And the police presence, still, as you can see...

COMPANY. **Have you seen this?**
Panic at the #BMEAwards

NEWS. 1. We're now being told... I'm hearing three –
    Three individuals have been admitted to hospital,
    Others being treated at the scene.

COMPANY. **Have you seen this?**
Dozens dead at the #BMEAwards

NEWS. 2. Two with minor – with fairly superficial –
    The third... No word on the third / individual, as of yet.

NEWS. 3. But we did, um, we did definitely hear shots fired –
    What sounded like shots being fired –

COMPANY. **Shots fired at the #BMEAwards**

NEWS. 3. Most people saying four or five, they think,
    As the last few guests were / making their way in.

NEWS. 1. No names have currently been released.
    They'll be waiting, of course, until the next-of-kin –
    Until they've made contact with the families.

The COMPANY *are googling search terms.*

COMPANY. **Who's at the #BMEAwards?**
Stars at the #BMEAwards

NEWS. 2. And we're hearing – we have heard / multiple
    reports –

NEWS. 3. But a lot of... of confusion, and / no real sense of –

NEWS. 1. But – yes – but we can now confirm
    That third victim in the most serious condition is –

The name is revealed. The REPORTERS *are reabsorbed as
the* COMPANY *swells forward.*

COMPANY. **Katie –**
    Katie –
    Katie –
    Katie –

    Reports that Katie Hopkins has –
    Why is Katie Hopkins now trending on – ?
    What's this latest thing with / Katie Hopkins?
    Katie Hopkins in the news again
    What has Katie Hopkins done this time?

    Katie!
    Katie!
    Katie!
    Katie!

    Katie Hopkins age
    Katie Hopkins family
    Katie Hopkins children

    Katie Hopkins fight
    Katie Hopkins controversy
    Katie Hopkins illness

    Katie!
    Katie!
    Katie!
    Katie!

    Katie Hopkins is a –
    Katie Hopkins should be –
    Katie Hopkins is no worse than –
    I totally agree with / Katie Hopkins
    Katie Hopkins is a professional troll
    Katie Hopkins doesn't have a –
    Katie Hopkins is playing a game

    Katie –
    Katie –

    Katie Hopkins should know when to –
    Katie Hopkins deserves to be –
    Katie Hopkins is a monster
    Katie Hopkins is a bully
    Katie Hopkins is my hero

Should be ignored
Should be knighted
Should be banned from Twitter
Should be left to drown just like the –
Should be free to say whatever she –
Should be prosecuted
Should be made Prime Minister
Should be brought to justice

Why are you all talking about Katie?
Why are we all so obsessed with Katie?
Can we all just stop indulging Katie?
What are all these statuses on Katie?

Katie!
Katie!
Katie!

Number ends.

2. The Hospital Vigil

A news jingle plays as we move from frenetic into sombre.
The slow beep of a heart monitor is incorporated into the score.

A NEWS ANCHOR *comes forward.*

ANCHOR. **Our top story tonight:**
    Police are describing a shooting in Central London
    As a deliberate assassination attempt
    On controversial public figure Katie Hopkins.
    Hopkins is understood to be under armed police
        protection
    At King's College Hospital in Camberwell,
    Where her condition remains critical.
    More updates, of course, as we get them.

The noise of the heart monitor ceases, signifying death.
The COMPANY *come together and deliver the following*
in unison.

REPORTERS. **Businesswoman, columnist and broadcaster**
     Katie Hopkins
     Today died at the age of forty-three,
     From injuries sustained last night
     At the British Media and Entertainment Awards.
     Police are treating this as a murder investigation.
     We are expecting a statement from her family later today.

3. In Other News...

One reporter, OWEN, *remains on stage.* SHAYMA *is watching this broadcast, holding a notepad and a TV remote.*

OWEN. In other news, the bodies of eleven men and women –

   SHAYMA *rewinds this moment and replays it.*

   In other news, the bodies of eleven men and women –

   SHAYMA *rewinds and replays again.*

   The bodies of eleven men and women –

   SHAYMA *rewinds and replays again. This time she lets it play.*

   Eleven men and women have been recovered
   From a static caravan near Dartford in Kent
   After a fire swept through the site.
   No word yet on whether the cause of the fire appears suspicious.
   The investigation continues.

   SHAYMA *stops the recording. She takes out her phone and makes a call. We hear the voicemail she leaves.*

SHAYMA. Elena, hi, it's Shayma – Shayma Hussaini, calling you back. Look, I've just been watching the um, the reports of the fire and it's just... And you are, are you, you're one hundred per cent sure your cousin is one of the...? Because they said they hadn't... Anyway, look, I'm going to try and help in whatever way I can, of course I will. Just... Just hang in there, okay? Okay.

4. Where Were You When?

Lights shift. Six members of the COMPANY *join* SHAYMA *and* OWEN *on stage. They are* KAYLEIGH, *a recent graduate,* PAM *and* RICHARD, *a couple,* BRIAN, *retired,* NINA, *a teacher,* KARL, *unemployed. There are no gaps here – all voices overlap.*

KAYLEIGH. Okay. Um. My name is Kayleigh Harris
    I work in the third sector – charity sector.
    Where would you like me to start?
    (*Beat.*) Right. Gosh. No, absolutely.
    On the night of her death?
    Uh. I would've been –

PAM. We were –

RICHARD. In Tescos, weren't we?

SHAYMA. Um, I'm not –

PAM (*correcting* RICHARD). Sainsbury's.

SHAYMA. Not sure.

PAM. We stopped going to Tesco's after –

RICHARD. Had we?

SHAYMA. Home. I think home. Yeah.

KARL. Just chilling, just on my phone.

BRIAN. Couldn't say.

KARL. Just scrolling through, and –

OWEN. You never know what's coming.

NINA. Not until the morning.
    Someone in the staffroom was –

OWEN. Every day is always –

KAYLEIGH. I had a text from Brandon.

KARL. Bam!

KAYLEIGH. That's my boyfriend – was my boyfriend –
    Brandon.

KARL. It was all, yeah it was mad –
    All kicking off like –

BRIAN. If I'm honest – being honest –
    I hadn't really heard of, um –

KAYLEIGH. He does this thing – like a running joke –
    Like a sort of… Not really a joke, but –
    He'll text 'so-and-so equals dead'.

SHAYMA. Because I was off work then. It was –

KAYLEIGH. 'David Bowie equals dead'

BRIAN. But I did, yes, I vaguely recognised –

KAYLEIGH. 'Bruce Forsyth equals dead'

NINA. Shocking. Yeah, quite genuinely shocking.

KAYLEIGH. Or 'Prince Charles equals dead' –
    And you never know if it's real, so –

OWEN. So first you have to verify it.

KARL. And I'm all just like 'no way mate.'

SHAYMA. I wasn't… I can't very clearly –

KAYLEIGH. I know it's not – no, it's not –
    It might sound a little –

RICHARD. We had a message from our Shona.

PAM. That's his sister, Shona –

RICHARD. Yes –

PAM. Sent a message to –

RICHARD. Because she knew we'd want to –
    As… Not as *fans*, but –

PAM. No, not fans, but actually more of –

SHAYMA. Look, there were other…
    So I wasn't very, um, what's the word?

PAM. Because she said, didn't she,
    What we were all thinking –
    What a lot of us were thinking –

BRIAN. But I didn't give her too much thought, I'm afraid.

SHAYMA. Sad. Not that it wasn't sad –

OWEN. But quickly – very quickly your brain just…
Things stop being surprising.
Not desensitised as such, but –

NINA. And the kids –

KARL. Mate, come on –

NINA. You don't know how they're going to take it –

KARL. Splat! Pow! Gone – just crazy.

SHAYMA. But I had my own…
So I was never going to lose sleep over…
That isn't what I mean to say, but –

KARL. Cos it takes – yeah it can take,
Don't straight away just…

KAYLEIGH. So I googled it, straight off –

NINA. They aren't always –

PAM. Admirable –

RICHARD. She always said that –

PAM. Admirable in that, in that sense of –

RICHARD. Admirable.

PAM. To be that person who will –

OWEN. Not *expected*, but a part of you just goes –

BRIAN. But she wasn't, uh, very well thought of, was she?
She had, um, quite a reputation –

OWEN. Okay.

KAYLEIGH. And yeah, there it was.

BRIAN. For getting on the wrong side of –

KARL. Cos it's weird, y'know?

BRIAN. Of, uh, in any number of instances –

OWEN. Which isn't –

SHAYMA. Because obviously – obviously it was awful.
    No question.

NINA. And I remember thinking… I – (*Laughs.*)
    And I shouldn't say this
    No, I don't think I should say this,
    But I remember just thinking
    It was a bit like the, um, the Agatha Christie –

BRIAN. People having their noses put out of joint by her.

NINA. Is it – uh – Orient Express?
    Where everyone's done it.

KAYLEIGH. Yeah. Real.

NINA. Because there were so many people –
    So many who would, well, y'know –

KARL. Then all these batshit crazy theories, like.

NINA. Would want her dead, I suppose.
    I'm sorry. No. That isn't funny.
    I didn't mean to…
    Sorry.

    We move into a fully sung moment. Same characters/setting.

5. Say the Unsayable

PAM. Because she said, didn't she,
    What we were all thinking
    What a lot of us were thinking
    A lot of people were, y'know,
    She made you think.

RICHARD. And I'm not – I'm really not
    I didn't agree with
    Didn't always agree with
    But even so you always need
    A person who will –

Others begin to join in gradually.

OTHERS. Say the unsayable!

PAM. You always need that person who will

OTHERS. Say the unsayable!

RICHARD. Won't ever make you popular but

OTHERS. Say the unsayable!

PAM. I mean that's what they paid her for but

ALL. Say the unsayable!

RICHARD. Not just to shock, but actually to –

KAYLEIGH. Because we're all – we can be
    We can be a little
    Yeah a lot of times a little
    A lot of times we can, y'know
    Be kind of harsh

KARL. Cos it takes – yeah it can take –

NINA. And I shouldn't say this –
    No I don't think I should say this –

PAM/RICHARD. But even so, you always need
    A person who will

ALL. Say the unsayable!

BRIAN. She had, um, quite a reputation –

ALL. Say the unsayable!

SHAYMA. That isn't what I mean to say, but –

ALL. Say the unsayable!

NINA. You don't know how they're going to take it –

ALL. Say the unsayable!

KARL. Then all these batshit crazy theories –

The following parts overlap.

ALL. I know it's not, no it's not
    No I'm not, I'm not
It might sound a little
    So I googled it straight off
Cos there were so many people
    And yeah, there it was
So many who would, well, y'know
Would want her dead

It was all, yeah it was mad
All kicking off like
And I'm all just like 'no way mate'
But even so,
I always said it's admirable to –

Say the unsayable!

SHAYMA. Obviously it was awful

ALL. Say the unsayable!

NINA. Sorry, no, that isn't funny

ALL. Say the unsayable!

OWEN. First you have to verify it

ALL. Say the unsayable!

KARL. Splat! Pow! Gone – just crazy

ALL. Say the unsayable!
Say the unsayable!
Say the unsayable!

PAM. **And who's going to say it now?**

All go except for SHAYMA, *who stays to make a telephone call.*

6. Twelve in the End

A recorded phone conversation between SHAYMA *and* BENEDICT, *an older male solicitor.*

BENEDICT. Hello?

SHAYMA. Benedict. Hi. It's / Shayma –

BENEDICT. Oh, Shayma. Thank / you –

SHAYMA. Hi.

BENEDICT. For calling back.

SHAYMA. Not at all. (*Beat.*) So / did you get my – ?

BENEDICT. So I just thought we could... Sorry.

SHAYMA. No, sorry – you go.

BENEDICT. So yes, so wonderful. So I did get your email. I've / had a –

SHAYMA. Great.

BENEDICT. Chance to... Oh, but before we... You know this, naturally, but just to say, to remind you we do record – we are recording these calls, just / to –

SHAYMA. Right.

BENEDICT. Just for everyone's benefit. Just so we're all –

SHAYMA. Yeah. Of course. I should probably... Can I get a copy of it too?

BENEDICT. Oh. Oh well I don't... Um. Let me look into... Anyway, let's not dwell on that. But you're well, are you? You are keeping well?

SHAYMA. I'm… Yeah, I'm… a bit cooped up. Itching to get back to it –

BENEDICT. Yes. No, of course. And I've got here – I've got your back-to-work assessment, big string of ticks from our end.

SHAYMA. Great.

BENEDICT. But it isn't… This is more about you, not us – about making sure you feel ready, and supported in whatever…

SHAYMA. Yeah. I think – sorry, can I – ?

BENEDICT. Please.

SHAYMA. I think really for me, the sooner the better, the sooner I can… And I know the, uh, the measures you've put in place, and just the fact that, um, that Mr Ashworth won't be there, is / really all –

BENEDICT. And I can assure –

SHAYMA. Yeah, so, so I think honestly I am – I'm in a good place to just dive back in, really.

BENEDICT. I see. Well, that's all very encouraging to hear, certainly.

SHAYMA. And I think… The other thing is – the other thing I mentioned in my email –

BENEDICT. Ah.

SHAYMA. You know, with / the –

BENEDICT. This is the fruit-pickers?

SHAYMA. Yeah, the –

BENEDICT. And that is… I don't –

SHAYMA. And it's just I think we could really… And time, obviously, is of the essence, so / I would –

BENEDICT. Yes. Yes, and not to… That is all… But I wouldn't worry too much about that for now. Let's try to prioritise –

SHAYMA. Has anybody spoken to Elena?

BENEDICT. Hmm?

SHAYMA. Elena? Um, Nicolescu – she's / the –

BENEDICT. Right – the – yes, of course. She's the cleaner?

SHAYMA. Yeah. And it's her, um, it's her cousin Alek – he was one of the, the victims. Of the fire. He was in the caravan.

BENEDICT. Yes. (*Beat.*) And she works for us?

SHAYMA. Yes, / she's –

BENEDICT. And you're friends?

SHAYMA. We're friendly, yeah. And all / this has –

BENEDICT. Yes. No, of course. And it really is… It's a testament to you that you're thinking about any of this, with everything else / that you've –

SHAYMA. I've just tried to –

BENEDICT. But listen, without sounding… This is a tragedy, obviously. Eleven, is it? Eleven people have died, / and that –

SHAYMA. Twelve.

BENEDICT. Sorry?

SHAYMA. Sorry. It was twelve in the end. They, um, the first reports said eleven but –

BENEDICT. Right.

SHAYMA. I think because of the, the uh, the state of the, um, the remains, / they –

BENEDICT. I see.

SHAYMA. With fires it can be hard to… So they missed one. Anyway. Sorry.

BENEDICT. Right. (*Beat.*) Look, I think… Thank you, first off – thank you for raising this. Leave it with us, but try not… And let's not make any more promises to, uh, to Ellie – Elena – until –

SHAYMA. I really haven't.

BENEDICT. Good – that's good. So here's what I'd like to do. I'd like to get you back in on a trial basis, on a reduced schedule, just as a temporary… to see how we go.

SHAYMA. Right.

BENEDICT. If you're happy – if you feel ready for that. / And then –

SHAYMA. Absolutely.

BENEDICT. Wonderful. So we'll get all that over to you in writing, within the next day or two –

SHAYMA. Thank you, really.

BENEDICT. Not at all. And as I say, try not to worry about the other thing. I'll let you get on. Take care now. Goodnight.

SHAYMA. Yes, and you. Goodnight.

They go.

7. Minutes from Humanity Strategy Meeting, 09.06.2018

A meeting room within the offices of Humanity, a Human Rights charity. Five employees from most senior to junior: REBEKAH, DAVID, CAROL, WESLEY *and* KAYLEIGH. *We see the dumbshow of their conversation for a moment, then* KAYLEIGH *presses record on a Dictaphone and we immediately hear the sound.*

DAVID. Total shit-show –

REBEKAH. Alright, let's / just try to –

DAVID. In death as in life.

REBEKAH. Please. A little order please. Kayleigh?

KAYLEIGH. Hmm?

CAROL (*to* KAYLEIGH). Is it recording?

KAYLEIGH *nods.*

DAVID. I think we can trust the intern to operate a Dictaphone.

REBEKAH. Right. I'm saying let's just get on top of this.

WESLEY. Nail something down now and issue / a – get out a –

CAROL. For?

REBEKAH. By / eleven.

WESLEY. Lunchtime. Yeah, / or –

CAROL. Uh-huh.

WESLEY. Soon as we can.

REBEKAH. Yep.

DAVID. Now hold on –

REBEKAH. We – I think a simple, a… straightforward –

DAVID. Let's all – let's just take a breath –

WESLEY. We can't miss –

DAVID. Why?

WESLEY. There's a window – a window in which to – a timely –

REBEKAH. We can't equivocate – be seen / to –

CAROL. No.

DAVID. Why should we…? We have our own – own agenda –
a, uh – Kayleigh, today – what're we meant to… what's on
the actual – ?

KAYLEIGH. We… um… We've got the fundraising review.
Uh. New, the new stats on the domestic violence campaign.
The fruit-pickers. / Uh –

REBEKAH. Alright, yes, thank / you, Kayleigh.

DAVID. So okay – so let's –

REBEKAH. And we will – we will get to / all of –

WESLEY. Who are the fruit-pickers?

KAYLEIGH. It's the, um, there was a fire? Here it is.
MacArthur Gledhill – big farmsite in Kent. A dozen migrant
workers died / in a –

DAVID. Right. Yes. This is my exact… Twelve people have – twelve defenceless… and we have to waste our breath on Katie Hopkins?

REBEKAH. They might, yes, just for this morning they might have to wait for a –

DAVID. This woman, she… Let's not beat around the bush – we weren't – we didn't – we wrote petitions against her – we / actually wrote –

CAROL. That wasn't –

DAVID. No – let me finish – reported her to… to… Filed complaints – incitement to… We can't / just suddenly –

REBEKAH. And yes – and okay – so that's why. We had previous. We were critical – highly critical, yes – and so that is why we… That doesn't make what's happened to her any less of a –

DAVID. Doesn't it?

REBEKAH. We are… We do Human Rights. She is human – was human – is still a… she still has rights – bottom line – and we… we have to call out wherever – especially where we… No one's saying she's a saint. We're just saying –

WESLEY. You don't have to like her to mourn her.

REBEKAH. Exactly.

CAROL (*to* KAYLEIGH). Don't write that down.

REBEKAH. You don't have to mourn her to acknowledge… to… to…

WESLEY. To acknowledge the… to be disgusted / by –

REBEKAH. Yes.

WESLEY. This is a – fundamentally – this is an issue, isn't it, of / free –

CAROL. Free speech.

WESLEY. Free speech – yes – which is a cornerstone / of any –

REBEKAH. Yes.

WESLEY. Fundamental – absolutely fundamental to a
democratic –

DAVID. We – yes – I mean yes – but *hate* speech –

CAROL. Let's not get –

REBEKAH. Nobody's saying hate speech.

DAVID. Why not?

REBEKAH. Because this is no time to –

DAVID. This is absolutely the time to… You… You… This is
a… Free speech isn't consequence-free speech – there are
outcomes – ramifications to constantly… Encouraging, yes –
goading – and I'm not saying she deserved it, and I'm not
cracking open the bubbly, but –

REBEKAH. But nothing.

CAROL. And we don't, just to – regarding motive – we don't
know –

REBEKAH. No. And let's… let's not overcomplicate this. All
we're saying is… What're we saying?

*Now as they start to construct their statement, music/rhythms
creep in. Part-sung.*

**However unpalatable her views might have been,
That is no / justification –**

CAROL. **I don't know if –**

REBEKAH. **Hmm?**

CAROL. **If… 'unpalatable', as a… given the…**

REBEKAH. **Though her views could be controversial –**

WESLEY. **To some.**

DAVID. **To many.**

REBEKAH. **Though many found her views –**

WESLEY. **Found *some* of her views –**

REBEKAH. **To be – on occasion – unpalatable –**

CAROL. **Controversial –**

WESLEY. **To some.**

DAVID. **To many!**

REBEKAH. **This is not a justification –**

WESLEY. **There can be no justification –**

CAROL. **Yes.**

REBEKAH. **Yes. For the… For the…**

WESLEY. **For this heinous –**

CAROL. **For the cowardly –**

REBEKAH. **For this – yes –**

WESLEY. **Yes –**

REBEKAH. **For this heinous and cowardly act of / violence –**

CAROL. **Wanton violence.**

REBEKAH. **Wanton violence. Nice.**

DAVID (*dryly, to* KAYLEIGH). **You getting all this?**

KAYLEIGH. **Uh-huh.**

REBEKAH. **So. Though her opinions were, on occasion –**

DAVID. **Always!**

WESLEY. **Sometimes.**

REBEKAH. **Though people did find her statements –**

CAROL. **Some of –**

DAVID. **Many!**

REBEKAH. **Though her views could be seen as sometimes –**

WESLEY. **That's not the issue.**

REBEKAH. **That is not the issue.**

CAROL. **There can be no justification.**

DAVID. Yeah, but –

REBEKAH. **There can be no justification**
For this heinous and cowardly act of wanton violence.

Pause.

Bit much?

WESLEY. No.

REBEKAH. Alright then – from the top:

They all chant/sing together.

ALL. **Though her views could be controversial**
And opinions were on occasion
This is still no justification –

Though some people did find her statements
And actions to be problematic
There can be no justification

There can be no justification
For this act of wanton violence

There can be no justification
For this heinous and cowardly
Act of wanton violence

If we want a civilised nation
There are certain basic principles
We must hold to be fundamental

And the right to voice an opinion
Without fear of violent reprisal
Must be held to be fundamental

There can be no justification
For this act of wanton violence

There can be no justification
For this heinous and cowardly
Act of wanton violence

REBEKAH *speaks.*

REBEKAH. Alright. Yes, that's it. Type it up. Get it out.

A VOICE *from the* COMPANY *appears to sing.*

VOICE 1. **Because she said, didn't she,**
What we were all thinking –

REBEKAH. And you know what, I think this is a
This is a test, to challenge some of our –
To try to, to understand why she –

A second VOICE *pops up.* REBEKAH *keeps talking over music.*

VOICE 2. **And I'm not – I'm really not**
I didn't agree with –
Didn't always agree with –

REBEKAH. Right – Kayleigh – this is what I want –
You're going to put together a Katie dossier
Give me a list of all the good stuff,
All the reasons – any not-totally-abhorrent reasons –
Why she chimed – anything positive –
Anything at all – anything that… Yeah? Good.
Because we should be trying to understand it –
We should be trying to… That's how we move forward.

ALL. **There can be no justification**
For this act of wanton violence

There can be no justification
For this heinous and cowardly
Act of wanton violence

Music ends.

8. The Katie Dossier

Others drift away and KAYLEIGH *comes forward, taking out her mobile phone. On a separate part of the stage,* BRANDON, *her boyfriend, comes forward, also on his phone. The conversation we hear takes place over WhatsApp.* KAYLEIGH *and* BRANDON *speak the text, and the* COMPANY *sing the emojis and actions (men singing* BRANDON's, *women* KAYLEIGH's).*

BRANDON. A Katie Dossier?

KAYLEIGH. Yep.

WOMEN. **Sick face emoji**

MEN. **crying with laughter**
 crying with laughter
 crying with laughter
 Brandon is typing

BRANDON. Seriously though, that's crazy
 R U going 2 do it?

WOMEN. **Kayleigh is typing**
 Kayleigh is typing
 Kayleigh is typing

KAYLEIGH. I guess I have to.

MEN. **Poop emoji**
 Skull and crossbones

KAYLEIGH. Be nice.

MEN. **Brandon is typing**
 Brandon is typing
 Brandon is typing
 Seventeen poop emojis – exclamation mark.

KAYLEIGH. Thx.

BRANDON. Like making the positive case for herpes.
 Do you want to come over?
 I can help.

MEN. **Eggplant emoji**

 KAYLEIGH *sighs and* BRANDON *goes.*

9. These Moments are Opportunities

KAYLEIGH *stays on stage and* SHAYMA *returns. They both speak to us.*

SHAYMA. I didn't hear 'no'. I wasn't told 'no' – I was told 'take it easy'.

KAYLEIGH. They… Actually most people just found it hilarious.

SHAYMA. And I don't really do that. I can't do that. So.

KAYLEIGH. Like, um, like it was such a preposterous thing –

SHAYMA. That wasn't an option.

KAYLEIGH. Just absolutely, just comically impossible.

SHAYMA. Because I needed to get back in –
And I needed to prove, to show them –

KAYLEIGH. To say anything nice. Find anything –

SHAYMA. Because look – who I was then – anyone who…
If you mentioned me – if you googled my name –

KAYLEIGH. And yeah, being honest, I wasn't sold on the idea either –

SHAYMA. I was just the girl who got felt up by her boss and then got him fired.

KAYLEIGH. Not at first –

SHAYMA. That was how… And there was still a lot of anger towards…
A lot of people felt that I, um, that I had…

KAYLEIGH. Because I wasn't a fan or a follower, or,
Or anything like that really.

SHAYMA. So I needed to change the narrative.
And I saw – with Elena – within that whole…
And yes, it was horrible, it was a…
But there was also an opportunity –

KAYLEIGH. I wasn't… That wasn't why I'd –

SHAYMA. These moments are opportunities.

KAYLEIGH. I signed up for domestic slavery, for sex
workers –

SHAYMA. You have wrongful death, you have migrant
workers –

KAYLEIGH. Women seeking refuge, women facing
discrimination –

SHAYMA. Zero-hour, uh, exploitation of the gig economy –

KAYLEIGH. Women who don't have the vote – Jesus!

SHAYMA. And a big Brexit narrative in there, definitely.

KAYLEIGH. I didn't take that job to champion Katie Hopkins.

SHAYMA. Y'know, just the most… this big, sexy, zeitgeisty –

KAYLEIGH. But – but ultimately – fundamentally –

SHAYMA. And it was right under their noses –

KAYLEIGH. She did deserve *something*, some kind of –
Just a basic…

SHAYMA. And I saw it – me. I knew.

KAYLEIGH. And you know what really got me? It was to
see people,
These supposedly compassionate, liberal, big-hearted…
Just descend into… well, ripping the piss really.

SHAYMA. I couldn't pass that up. I couldn't drop it.

KAYLEIGH. Making all these – tweeting all of these –
Horrible little, giggling, snickering little,
Schoolyard sort of… And passing it off as banter –
Y'know nudge-nudge wink-wink fucking banter. Sorry.

SHAYMA. And not just for me – for her too – and for all
of them –

KAYLEIGH. Because regardless of, of any prior, any
ideological…
What happened to her was just –

SHAYMA. All of the… Who suffered this –

KAYLEIGH. This unbelievably violent, this hateful, horrific –

SHAYMA. Just the most – the most awful imaginable –

KAYLEIGH. But because it was *her* –

SHAYMA. And those people don't always – because of who they are –

KAYLEIGH. People could still laugh – gloat – celebrate, even –

SHAYMA. They are so often… / And I couldn't allow that.

KAYLEIGH. And I couldn't allow that.
She deserved respect. Yeah, respect.

10. Glasgow Mardi Gras

KAYLEIGH *and* SHAYMA *go. A sense of a protest with a carnival/celebratory feel – drums and bright colours. The* COMPANY *here are Scottish revelers/protestors. They sing:*

COMPANY. **Katie, Katie, Katie!**
Dead, dead, dead!
Katie, Katie, Katie!
Dead, dead, dead!
Katie – dead!
Katie – dead!
Katie, Katie, Katie!
Dead, dead, dead!

Ding dong the bitch is dead!
So good riddance!
Aye good riddance!
Sing out the crazy bitch is dead!

Ding dong the bitch is dead!
Raise a glass
And kiss my ass!
Sing cos the crazy bitch is dead!

A REPORTER *speaks to us from the scene.*

REPORTER. Startling scenes in Glasgow tonight,
A mere twenty-four hours after the death
Of media personality Katie Hopkins
Where dozens of individuals have taken to the streets
Not to mourn, but to celebrate her passing.
Earlier today I spoke to some of the revellers
To ask what they hoped to achieve.

Four people, ADAM, GAVIN, TRACEY *and* DONNA,
emerge from the COMPANY.

ADAM. No, it's… listen. It's / not malicious. It's –

DONNA. It's – yeah – it's fun. / Just –

TRACEY. Just a day out.

DONNA. It's just – just a bit of fun. Just a / laugh, yeah.

GAVIN. Just a party.

ADAM. No, but / listen –

EWAN *lurches into shot, drunk, cheering.*

EWAN. Ding dong the bitch is dead!

ADAM. Listen. She… Yes – you could call it celebrating
It's our right to / celebrate.

EWAN. Free speech!

ADAM. She – at the end of the day –
She didn't like us – we didn't like her.

GAVIN. So good riddance!

TRACEY. Aye, good riddance / to the –

EWAN. Mess with Scotland, you get –

EWAN *mimes shooting a gun.*

ADAM. There's a serious point here.
She was given a platform –
You – the media – gave her a platform
To spew her hate. So now it's our turn

Not to… No, not to to hate, not to…
But to go on record. To be heard –
To – because we refuse to legitimise –
We / won't let –

EWAN. Ding dong the bitch is – like old Maggie
You remember Thatcher?
We had a – lit a bonfire.
How we did it up here. Burnt an effigy.

DONNA. She can do one.

The rest of the COMPANY *join them in song. A carnival/
Mardi Gras feel.*

COMPANY. **Ding dong the bitch is dead!**
So good riddance!
Aye good riddance!

Ding dong the bitch is dead!
Mess with Scotland you get –

It's just – just a bit of fun
Just a laugh yeah

It's just – just summat to do
Just a day out

Ding dong the bitch is dead!
So good riddance!
Aye good riddance!

Ding dong the bitch is dead!
Mess with Scotland you get –

It's just blowing off some steam
Not malicious

It's just – doesn't mean a thing
Just a party

And when they find him
Or her
Get yerself to Glasgow, son

Yeah when they find him
Or her
Never buy a pint again

We'll give him sanctuary
Like Mr WikiLeaks
Like what's-his-face – you know
Him at the Embassy

A little slice of Ecuador here on the Clyde
We'll find the stupid git somewhere to hide

It's just – it's a victory
It's catharsis

It's just – you remember it?
Just like Thatcher

Ding dong the bitch is dead!
So good riddance!
Aye good riddance!

Ding dong the bitch is dead!
Mess with Scotland you get –

It's just – it's a carnival
Wouldn't miss this

It's just – feels like Mardi Gras
'Cept it's freezing

Song ends. COMPANY *goes.*

11. Prime Minister's Questions

The PRIME MINISTER *addresses the House of Commons.*
Behind her, the COMPANY *form her front bench.*

PM. I did. I have seen the footage.
    And let me thank my honourable friend for raising it today.
    Although it's important to note
    This is a very small number –
    A tiny minority of individuals –
    We should still have no hesitation
    In labelling this incident appalling.
    Abhorrent.
    Utterly distasteful.
    This is not who we are.
    These are not our British values.
    This will not stand.
    I'm aware that Police Scotland have opened an investigation
    To ascertain whether any illegal activity has occurred,
    But whatever their findings, this behaviour is / disgraceful.

12. Je Suis Katie

The COMPANY *sing first as outraged politicians.*

COMPANY. **Disgraceful.**
    Yes this behaviour is disgraceful
    They do not represent our values
    I welcome this investigation

Now a shift as the COMPANY *start representing more*
online comments – tweets, Facebook statuses, vlog posts, etc.
Echoes of the opening Twitter chorus.

    Disgraceful.
    I think these fuckers are disgraceful
    I think they all should be arrested
    This lot are scum and should be dealt with

When the poor woman's dead
When she's still got her kids
When all she ever did was –

Cos she just spoke her mind
Put herself on the line
And all she ever did was –

Fearless.
Was singled out for being fearless
You know she'd have this lot for breakfast
A bunch of idiots and cowards

Thankful.
And you know what we should be thankful
That we had someone like her fighting
That we had someone like her with us

And what now, now she's gone?
Poor woman
She was right all along
Poor woman
And it's time we started

Cos she had a big gob
Poor woman
But she had a big heart
Poor woman
And it's time we started

Who's gonna speak up for Katie?
Who's gonna say it now?
Who's gonna speak up for Katie?
Who's gonna say it now?
Who's gonna speak up for Katie?
Who's gonna say it now?
Who's gonna speak up for Katie?
Who's gonna say it now?

Cos it's an outrage
And she needs us now so –

Je Suis Katie!
Je Suis Katie!

Cos it's an outrage
And we won't stand down so –

Je Suis Katie!
Je Suis Katie!

Cos it's an outrage
Cos it's mindless violence –

Je Suis Katie!
Je Suis Katie!

Cos it's an outrage
And we won't be silenced!

Je Suis Katie!
Je Suis Katie!
Je Suis Katie!
Je Suis Katie!

A big finish. Stage clears. A moment of silence.

13. The Memorial Service

A church hall – the memorial service for the deceased fruit-pickers mentioned in 'In Other News'. Music plays. Various MOURNERS *drift in, holding candles. Amongst them is* ELENA, *cousin of the deceased Alek, and* SHAYMA, *looking uncomfortable. As they enter, the names of the dead are sung.*

VOICE. **Alek Nicolescu. Andre Dalca. Aris Spiros.**
Camille Dobrescu. Reka Dobrescu. Mada Cutov.
Donna Zlatkov. Lexi Zlatkov. Nicole Moisil.
Peter Draganov. Sara Balan. Victor Groza.

ELENA *approaches a lectern to deliver her eulogy. The service is being filmed for the benefit of those relatives who can't be in the country. We could see this footage.*

ELENA. Hello. Good afternoon, um, my name is Elena.
Elena Nicolescu.
Alek was my cousin.

On a separate part of the stage, a SECRETARY *from* ELENA*'s work appears. They are not physically present at the memorial service, but sing as if they were.*

SECRETARY. **Dear Miss Nicolescu,**
Filmore Kaufman Kane is very sorry to hear of your loss.
In order to apply for compassionate leave, please supply
an authorised copy of the deceased's death certificate to
your HR representative.

We continue to cut between the eulogy and other voices.

ELENA. Um. He – we – uh, neither of us have much other, any other family here, but… but I know he felt – he thought of a lot of you here today as family.

SHAYMA. **Dear Elena,**
I am back now but we've got to go carefully
I'll do my best and I haven't forgotten
Just leave it with me.

ELENA. He was a good man. A kind man. Uh. And clever. He will be very cross if I don't remind you all how clever he was.

SECRETARY. **Dear Miss Nicolescu,**
Thank you for supplying the documents we requested.
Unfortunately compassionate leave can only be granted
following the death of an immediate family member,
classed as a parent, child or sibling.
Kind regards.

ELENA. I… uh… I'm sorry. I can't… You will understand I can't talk about Alek without talking a little about how he died. But that is…

SHAYMA. **Dear Elena,**
I think we should sit down and draw some questions up
But better to go slowly and try to be careful.
Just leave it with me.

ELENA. There is so much we don't know – that we are not being told. About the fire. How twelve people… How they could have…

DEBBIE, *another cleaner and colleague of* ELENA*'s, comes forward. She's very chirpy.*

DEBBIE. **Hiya Ellie,**
Yeah, I'll cover you on the twelfth – could use the cash.
Enjoy your holibobs – hope you're doing something nice.

ELENA. And those questions should be answered. They must
be. We, um, we have earned, we deserve those answers. I am
no one – only a cleaner – no one important, but I clean at a
law firm –

BENEDICT *comes forward.*

BENEDICT. **Dear Miss Nicolescu,**
It has come to our attention that you are still in dialogue
with one of our trainees, Shayma Hussaini. Miss Hussaini
has been advised that she does not have the time nor
expertise to assist you in this matter, and does not speak
on behalf of Filmore Kaufman Kane.

SECRETARY. **Dictated but not read.**

SHAYMA. **Dear Elena,**
No, it's not great but we've still got some options left
Still I'm not so sure I should come to the service
I'll leave it with you.

SHAYMA *now somewhat reluctantly joins the other*
MOURNERS, *clearly having been persuaded to attend.*
ELENA *singles her out.* SHAYMA *is uncomfortable with this.*

ELENA. My friend. Shayma Hussaini. Shayma is a lawyer –
a very clever lawyer from a very big firm. Filmore Kaufman
Kane. Very powerful. She is going to help us. We will have
justice. People will listen. They will not be forgotten. I…
We will not allow it.

14. A Strong, Unapologetic Woman

KAYLEIGH *comes forward. She is making a presentation to her colleagues.*

KAYLEIGH. Right. Alright, let's just... let's dive in, shall we?
So you all know what I've been...
Rebekah asked a question, and that was why –
Why did she, why did Katie have such a –
What was it about her that resonated?
Of course you jump online, and –

Behind her, the COMPANY *sing as a chorus of online* COMMENTERS.

COMPANY. **Call me racist too – I love Katie Hopkins**
Sorry fatties – I still love Katie Hopkins
Forget the snowflakes – I love Katie Hopkins

KAYLEIGH. She, she clearly tapped into something. So.
First off, she was a fighter – that's number one.
A powerful woman – a strong, unapologetic woman
Not a feminist. Not a feminist, no
But a strong woman on her own terms
Who – and this is absolutely true –
Got so much more shit, specifically gendered shit,
Than men who were saying just as bad or worse.
She was gobby in the way that women aren't meant to
be gobby
And she was punished for that.

One online VOICE *distinct from chorus.*

VOICE. And we always defend
Always quick to defend
To forgive to excuse
Y'know foreigners
All the immigrants
And the benefits – the claimants

KAYLEIGH. And so two – two is honesty. No, hear me out –
What was perceived as honesty. Unguarded. Unfiltered.
No equivocation or censorship or... She doesn't care –
didn't care –

Didn't wait to see which way the wind was blowing
Just bam and out there and people respond to that.

The rest of the COMPANY *join in.*

COMPANY. **And we always defend**
Always quick to defend
To forgive to excuse
Y'know foreigners
All the immigrants
And the benefits – the claimants

KAYLEIGH. Three: work ethic. She built this mini-empire, and,
And you know what, fought tooth and nail
To stay in the public eye, and okay, sure,
That didn't always look particularly dignified
But she was relentless. Undeniably.
She was shrewd, and clever, and…

COMPANY. **One: Powerful**
Two: Honesty
Three: Hard-working

KAYLEIGH. So that's four – four is clever
And five – funny. Properly witty
Even if you think it's cruel or sick or –
She gave as good as she got.
Six: Not a victim. That's key.

COMPANY. **Four: is clever**
Five: is funny
Six: Not a victim

KAYLEIGH. Because she could've been
With all her medical – the epilepsy –
And the constant attacks on…
But she wasn't. She was actually –

COMPANY. **A strong, unapologetic woman**
Doesn't care – didn't care –
Didn't wait to see

A strong unapologetic woman
Who was shrewd – who was smart –
Undeniably

KAYLEIGH. So that's, um, yeah, anyway,
    That's what I've come up with so far.

REBEKAH. Alright, yes, thank you Kayleigh.

Lights shift – the presentation is over. BRANDON *emerges,
sending a message.*

BRANDON. How did it go?

KAYLEIGH. Don't ask.

MEN. **crying with laughter**

BRANDON. Sorry

MEN. **crying sincerely**

He goes.

COMPANY. **Cos she just spoke the truth**
    And if you speak the truth
    Then they'll soon come for you
    They can't handle it
    They're not here for us
    Only help the ones who hate us.

Now KAYLEIGH *speaks to us again, as if being
interviewed.* COMPANY *sings underneath.*

KAYLEIGH. Honestly, I didn't plan any of it.
    I didn't sit down and…
    But the more that I… Because I took it seriously,
    I took my job seriously,
    And I take this – I take a woman's life seriously –
    I couldn't just… And she was –

COMPANY. **One: Powerful**
    Two: Honesty
    Three: Hard-working

    Four: is clever
    Five: is funny
    Six: Not a victim

As KAYLEIGH *finishes her speech she joins them to sing.*

COMPANY/KAYLEIGH. **A strong, unapologetic woman**
Doesn't care – didn't care –
Didn't wait to see

A strong unapologetic woman
Who was shrewd – who was smart –
Undeniably

Now KAYLEIGH *sings – the text is the mission statement*
from a website – we might see her composing it.

KAYLEIGH. **I'm frustrated by the double standards**
Of the liberal elite
Who think they can decide
Who's worthy of mourning.

I'm frustrated by the hypocrisy
Of the right-on lefties
Who want to pick and choose
The battles we're fighting

I am sick of violence, and excuses for violence
I am sick of men trying to silence women
And all I'm after is justice –
Justice for Katie

I am sick of men who will never listen,
And all I'm after is –

COMPANY. **Justice, justice, justice for Katie!**
Justice, justice, justice for Katie!

KAYLEIGH. **I am sick of jokes that aren't jokes**
And certainly aren't funny
And suggestions she somehow had it coming
And all I'm after is

COMPANY. **Justice, justice, justice for Katie!**
KAYLEIGH. **I am sick of hearing –**
COMPANY.   **Justice for Katie!**
KAYLEIGH. **Of the implication –**
COMPANY.   **Justice – justice for Katie!**
KAYLEIGH. **That because it's her she somehow deserves it**
Like she's not worthy of

COMPANY. **Justice, justice, justice, justice!**
    Justice, justice, justice for Katie!
    Justice, justice, justice for Katie!

Song ends. KAYLEIGH *and her supporters go.*

15. Your Future Endeavours

REBEKAH *comes forward with a letter. She reads it to us.*

REBEKAH. Dear Kayleigh,
    I just wanted to write to you personally to thank you for all
    your hard work with us here. I know it's deeply
    disappointing that we can't renew your contract, but as
    you're aware we're having to make cutbacks in all areas.
    I do hope that our paths will cross again.
    Wishing you the very best in all your future endeavours,
    Yours –

She goes.

16. A Moment of Your Time

SHAYMA *and* KAYLEIGH *occupy different areas of the stage.
Both hold recording apparatus and are trying to conduct
interviews.* KAYLEIGH *is in a town centre,* SHAYMA *is
outside the offices of McArthur Gledhill in Kent. Various
members of the* COMPANY *pass them as they try to grab
a word. They overlap.*

SHAYMA. Hello. Hi.
    My name is Shayma Hussaini
    I was hoping… I…

KAYLEIGH. Excuse me, hello,
    Have you got a minute
    To talk about a new – ?

SHAYMA. Hi. Hello there.
    My name is Shayma Hussaini –
    I'm a law student, and I wondered –

KAYLEIGH. Hiya. Alright?
    I'm Kayleigh, what's your name?
    No? No bother –

SHAYMA. Hello. Excuse me –
    Is it Mr Ferguson?
    I recognised you from the website –
    My name is Shayma Hussaini –
    I did email –

KAYLEIGH. No, what it is, is, we are a charity
    But I'm not asking for money
    I'm not, I promise!

SHAYMA. Hello – hi there – good morning!
    My name is Shayma Hussaini –
    I'm a solicitor – trainee solicitor –
    I'm looking into the –

    KAYLEIGH *has got someone to stop.*

KAYLEIGH. We are, yeah, we're Justice 4 Katie –
    We're a new women's charity, and –

MAN. Katie who?

KAYLEIGH. Katie Hopkins. But / we also –

MAN. Oh fuck off.

    He goes. SHAYMA *corners someone else.*

SHAYMA. Thank you. Thank you so much.
    I just need a moment of your time.
    I'm from Filmore Kaufman Kane,
    We're looking into the fire –

    Now they go. SHAYMA *shouts after them.*

    This isn't going away – I'm not going away!

    She looks around, sighs, checks her watch.

KAYLEIGH. Anyone? Hello? Anyone want to talk to me?

SHAYMA. Hello?

KAYLEIGH. Hello-o?

TOGETHER. Hello!

They go.

17. Hello YouTube

Four vloggers, DWIGHT, *an angry American,* FRANKIE,
a teen beauty blogger, MAX, *a somewhat geeky guy and* ISSY,
a would-be life coach.

DWIGHT. **Hello YouTube**
  Thanks for tuning in

FRANKIE. **Hello YouTube**
  Lots to chat about

MAX. **Hello YouTube**
  Big update this week

ISSY. **Hello YouTube**
  Please forgive the mess

ALL. **Gonna keep this quick**
  But please stick with me!

DWIGHT. Katie Hopkins – she is –
  She's like British royalty
  Not *actual* royalty, which they also have
  I know. Don't get me started.

FRANKIE. Your girl Frankie here,
  Getting serious for a minute
  Serious voice – ahem –
  Too serious?

MAX. Max to the Max
  Gonna chat through Marvel's big announcement –
  Lots of Comic-Con rumours to break down
  But before all that –

ISSY. I am scared, okay. I'm sorry but I am –
    That's why I needed to make this
    Because I am terrified.

ALL. **Hello YouTube**
    This is serious
    Hello YouTube
    I am terrified
    Gonna keep this quick
    But please stick with me

FRANKIE. I don't – you know I don't do politics –
    I don't want to upset anyone, but –

DWIGHT. How does this happen? Seriously?

MAX. This was an act of war –
    You all understand that, right?
    This is not normal.

ISSY. This is my office, and just look –
    Look out of the window –
    This is how close I was.

DWIGHT. Britain has fallen
    Britain is under Sharia law right now,
    Because they gave up their guns,
    And the question you've got to ask yourself now is –

    The rest of the COMPANY *join in.*

COMPANY. **How should we remember Katie Hopkins?**
    We must remember
    Don't get me started

    How should we remember Katie Hopkins?
    Got to get real now
    Can't be distorted

    And I think that as a mother
    And I think it's easy to forget
    And I think that as a fighter
    And at least she lived with no regrets

    And I think she was a saviour
    And I think that even though she's gone

And I don't think this is over
I think the worst is still to come

How should we remember Katie Hopkins?
Can't be forgotten
We'll find the bastards

How should we remember Katie Hopkins?
Time to take action
We'll make 'em suffer

Like and subscribe
Like and subscribe
Leave me a comment below

Like and subscribe
Like and subscribe
What do you think – let me know

Click to show respects
And better stick with me!

Song ends. They go, replaced by a more sombre
REPORTER.

REPORTER. Media personalities, reality-TV stars,
    Even Peers of the Realm;
    Just a few of the famous faces present
    At today's London memorial service
    For controversial public figure Katie Hopkins.
    While Downing Street confirmed
    The Prime Minister would not be in attendance,
    Citing prior commitments,
    We are expecting a fuller statement later today.

18. The Diana Moment

Two former advisers to Tony Blair, HARRIS *and* DELANEY, *are being interviewed.*

HARRIS. Of course it would've been / a –

DELANEY. Carnage –

HARRIS. Chaos, / absolutely.

DELANEY. Behind the scenes.

HARRIS. In those situations it's always, um, is it… what / is it?

DELANEY. Tricky to –

HARRIS. No, but what's the…? Is it ducks? On the surface you're –

DELANEY. Swans!

HARRIS. Swans! Yes! On the, yes, on the surface you're all serene and / gliding, but –

DELANEY. That's the idea.

HARRIS. Yes, but underneath it's always… And there's us – trying to craft the swan.

DELANEY. Of course Tony – Tony / was –

HARRIS. A natural.

DELANEY. Very swan-like already, yes.

HARRIS. Like a, um, like a duck to water, as it happens. (*Laughs.*) Uh…

DELANEY. But, uh, but no, but of course that was never her… her strongest…

HARRIS. And of course you have to remember at that point Katie wasn't… Nobody thought…
Her presence could still be seen as –

DELANEY. Toxic.

HARRIS. Absolutely. There wasn't a cut-and-dry…
Wasn't an obvious line.

DELANEY. And again, as we know, big public outpourings,
    Anything that requires, uh…

HARRIS. Human emotion.

    DELANEY *laughs*.

    Sorry.

DELANEY. But yes, but this is the… She always struggled
    with…
    And she would've been acutely aware –
    They would've sat her down and made her watch Tony.

HARRIS. Oh, undoubtedly.

DELANEY. You know, and his whole – the Diana moment –

HARRIS. Yes.

DELANEY. And that's, you know, it's unfair,
    Because it's not comparable – not really comparable –
    But because he was really seen to, to,
    To get it so right – really lock into the –

HARRIS. The public –

DELANEY. Public consciousness. Yes.

HARRIS. She would've been under immense pressure
    And everything – everything in that scenario is scrutinised –
    Every phrase – every word –

DELANEY. 'Speaking as a woman.'

HARRIS. Oh God, yes.

DELANEY. Because do you, do you…?
    You do those calculations
    'Does it help me to be a woman today?'

HARRIS. It sounds ridiculous, but –

DELANEY. No, but it's crucial –
    The tone you set in those moments is crucial, believe me.

    The PRIME MINISTER *comes forward to deliver her
    public eulogy.*

PM. I come here today, like so many others
    To pay my respects, and mourn the loss
    Of a crucial voice in our national debate.
    For all her controversies, in many ways
    Katie Hopkins represented the very best of Britain.
    Proud. Fearless. Articulate.
    Independent and enterprising.
    Utterly assured of her convictions,
    Never prepared to back down,
    Never asking for sympathy or handouts.
    We may not have always agreed,
    But let us be clear. Katie Hopkins is not –
    Has never been – the enemy.
    Her enemy is the enemy of us all –
    The enemy of free and open speech.
    Speaking as a woman –
    And speaking as a 'bloody difficult woman' at that –
    Let me say this:
    I want to live in Katie's Britain –
    A Britain where the brave speak freely,
    And the cowards who would silence them
    Are swiftly brought to justice.
    Our thoughts, of course, are with her family,
    And to them I give my personal assurances
    That those responsible shall be found
    And prosecuted to the full extent of the law,
    That these people can never, shall never, will never win,
    And there is no place for them
    In the Britain we are building.

    She goes.

19. Katie's Britain

Full COMPANY *come together.*

COMPANY. **I want to live in Katie's Britain.**
A Britain where the brave speak freely

Je Suis Katie! Je Suis Katie!

I want to live in Katie's Britain.
A Britain where the brave speak freely

Proud. Fearless. Articulate.

I want to live in Katie's Britain.
And those responsible shall be found.

Je Suis Katie! Je Suis Katie!

I want to live in Katie's Britain
And there is no place for them
No place for them
No place for them
In the Britain we are building.

SHAYMA *enters. She is still door-stepping workers in Kent,*
with little success. Throughout this, the COMPANY *swell*
forward as Katie's supporters, their movement gaining
strength and momentum.

SHAYMA. **Hello. Hi.**
How are you today?
My name is Shayma Hussaini.
I'm a law student.
I was wondering –

COMPANY. **I want to live in Katie's Britain!**
A Britain where the brave speak freely

SHAYMA. **Hello. Hi.**
This won't take a mo –
My name is Shayma Hussaini.
I'm a law student.
I was wondering
If I could ask you some questions

COMPANY. **I want to live in Katie's Britain!**
Our thoughts of course are with her family

Now we see KAYLEIGH *as well. She is doing much better.*
The verses overlap.

SHAYMA. **Hello. Hi.**
KAYLEIGH.   **Hello. Hi.**
SHAYMA. **What a lovely day.**
KAYLEIGH.   **Yes that's right I am –**
SHAYMA. **My name is Shayma Hussaini.**
KAYLEIGH.   **Yes I'm from Justice 4 Katie –**
SHAYMA. **I'm a law student.**
KAYLEIGH.   **Katie Hopkins**
SHAYMA. **I was wondering**
KAYLEIGH. **So you've heard of us?**

SHAYMA. **If I could ask you some questions**
    About McArthur Gledhill, and –

COMPANY. **Proud, fearless, articulate!**
    And those responsible shall be found
    Je Suis Katie!

SHAYMA. **Hello. Hi.**
KAYLEIGH.   **Hello. Hi.**
SHAYMA. **Getting chilly now.**
KAYLEIGH.   **Thanks for calling back**
SHAYMA. **My name is Shayma Hussaini.**
KAYLEIGH.   **Yes, I'm the one that you spoke to**
SHAYMA. **I'm a law student.**
KAYLEIGH.   **Yes I'd love that**
SHAYMA. **I've been sent here to**
KAYLEIGH.   **We can do this**
SHAYMA. **So I can ask you some questions**
KAYLEIGH.   **It really is all about justice –**
SHAYMA. **About McArthur Gledhill –**
KAYLEIGH.   **And protecting our freedoms**
SHAYMA. **And the immigrants, that's right.**
    It's really –

COMPANY. **And shall be swiftly brought to justice**
    Proud! Proud!
    Justice for Katie!

SHAYMA. **Hello. Hi.**
KAYLEIGH. **Hello. Hi.**

SHAYMA. **Gosh, it's fierce out!**
KAYLEIGH. **Let me write this down –**
SHAYMA. **My name is Shayma Hussaini.**
I'm a... solicitor.

KAYLEIGH *goes*. BENEDICT *now appears from the* COMPANY.

SHAYMA. **I've been sent here to ask you some questions**
BENEDICT.   **Shayma we have given you some leeway –**
SHAYMA. **About McArthur Gledhill, and –**
And the fire here, that's right
BENEDICT.   **It's a little disturbing**
SHAYMA. **It's really very important –**
BENEDICT.   **It's really very concerning**
SHAYMA. **It really won't take a minute –**
BENEDICT.   **I really have to insist you –**
SHAYMA. **I swear, I'm out of your hair in –**

KAYLEIGH *returns briefly, in a triumphant mood.*

COMPANY. **I want to live in Katie's Britain**
And there is no place for them
KAYLEIGH.   **I'll get that to you now**
COMPANY. **No place for them**
KAYLEIGH.   **No, I won't let you down**
COMPANY. **No place for them**
KAYLEIGH.   **We're going to make her proud**
COMPANY. **In the Britain we are building.**

KAYLEIGH *goes*.

SHAYMA. Yes, of course. Well, just think about it.

Music shifts, coming down to something less bombastic.

Dear Benedict,
I take your point and I totally get that
And I promise you I am being careful
But if you'll let me –

BENEDICT. Dear Shayma,
There is no question in my mind that your intentions are
honourable, and Filmore Kaufman Kane will always
encourage initiative where appropriate. However –

SHAYMA*'s reply feels more pointed – steelier.*

SHAYMA. **Dear Benedict,**
It means so much that you're here to support me
Especially with everything I've been through
Just leave it with me.

BENEDICT. Dear Miss Hussaini,
Please note that we are in no way opening an official casefile
on the McArthur Gledhill fire. If you must proceed, tread
very carefully.
Regards.

BENEDICT *goes, clearly unhappy.* SHAYMA *smiles and
leaves too.*

20. One of Us

A snippet from a radio news bulletin is heard.

RADIO.... growing frustration that despite the Prime Minister's
assurances no arrests have yet been made. Mr Addison
claimed that there would be 'rioting on the streets' if the
police weren't able to produce a suspect soon.

Three figures, FAHAD, DIPO *and* MARIAM, *come forward
as if being interviewed.*

DIPO. **And there was a sense**
Yes there was a sense
Just a sort of unspoken
Just a general sort of sense of
An awareness things could

MARIAM. **And there was a sense**
Yes there was a sense
Yes a very uneasy
Just a general sort of sense that
Any moment things could

FAHAD. **And there was a sense**
Yes there was a sense

Just a – hardly surprising
Just a very natural sense that
Very likely things could

ALL. **Oh please God don't let it**
Don't let it be one of you know
One of us

Oh please God don't let it
Don't let it be one of you know
One of us

Oh fuck please let it – let it be someone
You know – someone white

Fuck but fuck please let it be someone
You know – someone white

Oh fuck please let it – let it be someone
You know – someone white

Fuck but fuck please let it be someone
You know – someone white

Some white nutter and it won't matter then
Some white nutter who's just – some crazy

Some white nutter and that would be great
Some white nutter and I'd sleep easy

FAHAD. **Not being funny but**

MARIAM. **Not being funny or**

DIPO. **Not being funny just**

ALL. **Some white nutter and they'll quickly forget**
Some white nutter and they'll soon leave it

Some white nutter and that would be fine
No one ever puts 'white' in the headline

Oh please God don't let it
Don't let it be one of you know –

An abrupt cut-off. A REPORTER *appears.*

REPORTER. Police are looking for a British Asian male
Wanted in connection with the death

Of television personality Katie Hopkins.
The suspect is believed to be
Tall, bearded and in his mid-thirties.

ALL. Fuck.

21. Tall, Bearded and in His Mid-Thirties

The rest of the COMPANY *return as the members of the public.
First we hear individual voices that gradually build and come
together.*

COMPANY. **Tall, bearded and in his mid-thirties**
  Course he's one of them
  Heard Somalian
  Syrian
  One of them
  One of the usual suspects

  Tall, bearded and in his mid-thirties
  Know he's one of those
  Some Jihadi bloke
  Radical
  One of those
  We should've seen it coming

  Oh but course they'll string you up
  String you up for saying that
  Cos you can't say anything
  When it's him they should be lynching

  Tall, bearded and in his mid-thirties
  Well we might've guessed
  We'd have thought no less
  What a mess!
  Might've guessed
  We should've seen it coming

  Tall, bearded and in his mid-thirties
  What would you expect?
  Bet nobody checked

So what next?
So what now?
Somebody must do something

Oh but ain't it typical
Just what I was telling you
Yeah they always look the same
Though you're not allowed to say it

And we always defend
Always quick to defend
To forgive to excuse
Y'know foreigners
All the immigrants
And the benefits – the claimants

22. Interview with Beyoncé Knowles

A café. SHAYMA *is sat with* CATALINA, *a Romanian fruit-picker. The conversation begins as* SHAYMA *presses record on her Dictaphone, which she places on the table.*

SHAYMA. That's all running now.

CATALINA. Hmm?

SHAYMA. Recording. Just for my –

CATALINA. Right.

SHAYMA. My record. My… So you don't have to worry about –

CATALINA. You need to – ?

SHAYMA. Just for me. So I can keep a track of… No one else will –

CATALINA (*unsure*). Okay.

SHAYMA. And I really am… I know this is… I'm very grateful that you're talking to me.

CATALINA *nods.*

So… If you could. What'd be great is if you can just say your name, so that when I play it back I know… Again – just for me. Yeah?

CATALINA. I'm just… I am not meant to be –

SHAYMA. I know. Me neither really, but –

CATALINA. At the farm… If they knew that I was –

SHAYMA. Yeah. No, I get that, course I do. But this is… Those people, the people who… They were your mates, weren't they? Your friends?

CATALINA. Yes.

SHAYMA. So you want to make sure –

CATALINA. I do, but –

SHAYMA. You don't want them to get away with it.

CATALINA. No.

SHAYMA. Okay. So okay, why don't we… What if for now you could use a fake name?

CATALINA. Yes?

SHAYMA. Yeah. You could… As long as I know who…

CATALINA. Pick a name?

SHAYMA. Sure.

CATALINA. Like a spy?

SHAYMA. Uh-huh. Anything you like. Anything… Better, yeah?

CATALINA. Anything?

SHAYMA. Anything at all. So… okay, so July 18th, 2018 – commencing interview with…

CATALINA (*leaning towards the microphone*). Beyoncé Knowles.

SHAYMA (*laughs*). Okay… Great. Yeah. So, Miss Knowles…

CATALINA (*giggling too*). Please, call me Bey.

SHAYMA. So, Bey. Great. Why don't you –

A number of rowdy football FANS *enter the café, singing.*

FANS. **I'm England 'til I die! I'm England 'til I die!**
I know I am, I'm sure I am,
I'm England 'til I die!

SHAYMA. Tell you what – why don't we find somewhere a bit
quieter?

CATALINA *nods, relieved.* SHAYMA *leans forward to stop*
her recording. Snap blackout as she turns the Dictaphone
off. Sound of drums, and the singing increases.

23. England 'til I Die

The café disappears. The FANS *are joined by the rest of the*
COMPANY, *now part of a vigil/protest. They carry placards*
with 'Justice for Katie' and other similar slogans. Amongst
them, a number of different REPORTERS.

COMPANY. **I'm England 'til I die! I'm England 'til I die!**
I know I am, I'm sure I am,
I'm England 'til I die!

And we always defend
Always quick to defend
To forgive to excuse
Y'know foreigners
        Justice for Katie!
All the immigrants
        Justice for Katie!
And the benefits – the claimants

REPORTER. March organisers claim they expect
Tens of thousands of people
To attend a candlelit vigil for Katie Hopkins
In Trafalgar Square later this evening

COMPANY. **I want to live in Katie's Britain –**
A Britain where the brave speak freely!

REPORTER. This is a tribute, they say, nothing more
But commenters on social media
Seem to believe revolution is in the air –

Aside, KAYLEIGH *appears to be practising her lines.*

KAYLEIGH. **One: Powerful**
Two: Honesty
Three: Hard-working

Four: is clever
Five: is funny
Six: Not a victim

COMPANY. **I want to live in Katie's Britain –**
A Britain where the brave speak freely!

Cos she just spoke her mind
Poor woman
Put herself on the line
Poor woman
And all she ever did was –

The REPORTER *now talks to the audience as if being interviewed, rather than presenting.*

REPORTER. If you know the quote you want you can literally put the words in people's mouths – it's almost like a Derren Brown thing. So I – I can say to someone something like – (*Turning to a protestor.*) 'Katie Hopkins was an icon, wasn't she?' and they go:

PROTESTER. Yeah Katie Hopkins *was* an icon.

REPORTER (*to audience*). I cut the 'yeah' and:

PROTESTOR. Katie Hopkins *was* an icon.

REPORTER. Bingo. That's the line I needed, right there on tape – the public call Katie Hopkins / an icon.

REPORTER *goes.*

COMPANY. **An icon**
Yeah of course she was an icon
Katie Hopkins was an icon

And she will never be forgotten!
And she will never be forgotten!
And she will never be forgotten!

I want to live, I want to live,
I want to live in –

I'm England 'til, I'm England 'til,
I'm England 'til I die

SHAYMA *crosses the stage leaving a voicemail.*

SHAYMA. Catalina, hi –
I mean Beyoncé, sorry –
Did you make it on your train?
The centre here is crazy

She goes.

24. Fazil Mohammed

Another NEWSREADER *appears.*

NEWS. Tensions were further raised as police released the
name of Fazil Mohammed –

The COMPANY *sing as if entering a search term.*

COMPANY. **Fazil Mohammed!**

NEWS. A thirty-four-year-old plasterer from –

COMPANY. **Fazil Mohammed plasterer**

NEWS. Mr Mohammed was last seen in the Marylebone area
on the –

COMPANY. **Fazil Mohammed Marylebone**

NEWS. But is believed to have left the country. Family
members in Wembley say –

COMPANY. **Fazil Mohammed Wembley!**

A chime to suggest a positive result has been found.

**Fazil Mohammed GDC
Painless Dentistry
Wembley!**

The COMPANY *try searching again.*

Fazil Mohammed plasterer Wembley

A sound to suggest no fitting results.

Fazil Mohammed handyman Wembley

The same.

Fazil Mohammed Wembley?

The positive chime again. Into a cheerful jingle from a radio advert.

JINGLE. **Smile bright, smile white
We can make your smile right!**

FAZIL *comes forward, a part of his cheesy advert. He wears a dentist's smock.*

FAZIL. With prices to suit all pockets, I promise I'll give *you* something to smile about.

A message is sent around the PROTESTERS.

COMPANY. **RobG liked this
Tanya Davis pinned this
England's Army posted this –**

KAYLEIGH *sees the message. She presses a button and the music swells.*

Kayleigh Harris shared this!

They all receive it.

**Found him!
Found him!
Got him!
Found him!
Swear to God we've found him!
Look at this they've found him!**

**Tall, bearded and in his mid-thirties
It's just like we thought**

Share this news report
Get him caught
Like we thought
Let him be taught a lesson

New terms are searched for.

Fazil Mohammed GDC
Dr Fazil Mohammed – Wembley

Another chime – a BLOGGER *appears.*

BLOGGER. And huge thanks to the good doctor Fazil
Mohammed for hosting this month's Wembley Bookworms –
a lively discussion was –

COMPANY. **Found him!**
Found him!
Got him!
Found him!
136 Harrowdene Road!

Found him!
Found him!
Got him!
Found him!
136 Harrowdene Road!

JINGLE. **Smile bright, smile white**
We can make your smile right!

SHAYMA *appears again.*

SHAYMA. **Catalina, hi**
I'm just checking you got home
Thanks again for finding time
The streets tonight feel pretty ugly.

*She goes. We now see more messages/map locations/other
information continuing to be shared. The* COMPANY
*gradually come forward from the back of the stage, now
feeling more like a mob. We get the impression of hundreds
of people, all wearing rubber Katie Hopkins masks.*

COMPANY. **Justice, justice, justice for Katie!**
Justice, justice, justice for Katie!

No one here was saying violence, were they?
But still sometimes
Sometimes you can't

No, no one ever wanted violence, did they?
But still sometimes
You can't help if –

VOICE 1. I'd love to get my hands on him
I'd love to – just five minutes yeah
Five minutes yeah and lock the door
I'd show you something special

COMPANY. **I'd love to get my hands on him**
I'd love to – just five minutes yeah
Five minutes yeah and lock the door
I'd show you something special

JINGLE. **We can make your smile right!**

KAYLEIGH *addresses the crowds in Trafalgar Square.*
She smiles widely.

KAYLEIGH. Why am I smiling?
Why am I smiling on such a day of tragedy and anger?
Because I am amongst friends
And because today we are taking action

COMPANY. **Justice, justice, justice for Katie!**

No, no one ever wanted violence, did they?
Still can't help if
There's some fallout

No, no one ever wanted violence, did they?
No one wanted
Nor did Katie

And you can't lose sleep over something like that
And you can't lose sleep cos that's how they get you

You can't um – what's the thing that they say?
Um, omelettes – without breaking

No, no one ever wanted violence, did they?
It's a shame, but
Who can help it?

KAYLEIGH. We're not a political movement
COMPANY. **This is about the people**

KAYLEIGH. We're not a political movement
COMPANY. **This is about compassion**

KAYLEIGH. We're not a political movement
COMPANY. **This is a search for justice**

    Justice, justice, justice for Katie!
    Justice, justice, justice for Katie!

KAYLEIGH. **This is about ensuring**
    Our rights will be protected

    This is about ensuring
    All women are respected

    This is about a search for
    A permanent solution

    This is not a political movement
    This is a revolution.

The rest of the COMPANY *now join her.*

KAYLEIGH/COMPANY. **This is about rejecting**
    A system that has failed us

    This is about reclaiming
    A country that was stolen

    This is an affirmation
    Of our beliefs and values

    We're not a political movement
    This is a revolution.

    We're not a political movement
    This is a revolution

VOICE **Five minutes yeah and lock the door**
    I'll show you something special

FAZIL. I promise, I'll give *you* something to smile about.

End of Act One.

ACT TWO

1. Entr'acte

The second act starts in a similar fashion to the first – a series of tweets, comments, reports and headlines, some sung, some spoken.

COMPANY. **Have you seen this?**
A bunch of animals
Have you seen this?
Don't believe a word of it

Have you seen this?
That report is bullshit
Share this link from @DeathToVegans

Have you seen this?
'Hopkins vigil marred by violence'

Have you seen this?
'Mistaken identity leaves dentist hospitalised'

COMMENT. Bawling my eyes out over this – can't believe this is my country.

COMMENT. He had it coming – just look at him. #no-smoke-without-fire

COMPANY. **Have you seen this?**
'Vigil victim seeks compensation'

Have you seen this?
'Migrant doctor's tax-scam shame'

KAYLEIGH *appears*.

KAYLEIGH. **Have you had a chance to read the last update**
I sent?
I think there's lots still to say
I still have a lot to say –

She goes.

COMPANY. **Who's gonna speak up for Katie?**
Who's gonna say it now?
Who's gonna stand up for Katie?
Who's gonna say it now?

Have you seen this?
'Hopkins statue petition provokes online ridicule'

Have you seen this?
'The Ten stupidest things we heard at the J4K rally'

Disgusting!
This piece is totally disgusting!
I can't believe that people can be –
It makes me sick right to my stomach!

SHAYMA *appears.*

SHAYMA. **Has anybody seen the coroner's report yet?**
There's so much they're not telling us.

She goes.

COMPANY. **Have you seen this?**
Police arrest the real Fazil Mohammed

Have you seen this?
Now we'll finally get some justice!

A police SPOKESPERSON *emerges – a snippet from a press
conference.*

SPOKES. We can... thank you. We can confirm, yes,
That we recently brought in a suspect for questioning
However, this individual has been released without charge
And forms no part of our ongoing investigation –

They go.

TWEET. What a joke – you know he must've done something.

COMPANY. **Annabel Ross and six others like this**

TWEET. Another victory for the PC brigade. #no-justice

COMPANY. **Mickey O'Keefe and twenty-nine others**
retweeted this

COMPANY. **Have you seen this?**
Was it really six months ago – have you seen this?

HEADLINE. On the six-month anniversary of her death, six of our writers reflect on –

TWEET. **RIP Katie – still in our thoughts. #never-forgotten.**
RIP Katie – still in our thoughts. #never-forgotten.

HEADLINE. Is the Commentariat in crisis? Max Anderson argues –

HEADLINE. Is *TOWIE*'s Kimberley Newport the new Katie Hopkins?

HEADLINE. Is Britain ready to embrace a kinder discourse?

COMPANY. **Have you seen this simple trick to lose ten pounds in ten days?**
Have you seen what Sia wore to the MET on Friday night?
Have you seen what happens when these lions are reunited?

Have you seen this?
Have you seen this?
Have you seen?

Song ends.

2. Empathy Exhaustion

A split scene, KAYLEIGH *on one side of the stage,* FAZIL *on the other.* FAZIL *speaks,* KAYLEIGH *sings.*

FAZIL. Hello. One-two. Yes. I am Fazil Mohammed.
Um. One of the Fazil Mohammeds.
I'm the dentist. I'm still a dentist, yes.

KAYLEIGH. **We call it empathy exhaustion.**
Um. Yeah. Empathy exhaustion.
Cos it's a battle – a real battle, y'know

And there's always so much clamouring
Lot of shouting and clamouring
Too much happening – to keep track of it, y'know.

FAZIL. Some of the images, they, they uh, stick with you.
Like the masks. The plastic, uh – no, not plastic
I think rubber, actually – masks of her face
Like Halloween – like trick-or-treat.

KAYLEIGH. **And it's not that**
It's not that
That people don't care

No it's not that
It's not that
That people don't care

But there's a lot going on and it's tough
Can be tough to hang in there.

FAZIL. All, uh, all just lined up, bunched up on the doorstep.
Almost funny. Um. I think I might've –
I laughed, because it was so… Just…

SHAYMA *enters leaving a voicemail on her mobile.*

SHAYMA. **Hi Catalina**
I know it's been a while
And you've been having issues with your phone
And – I don't know – I've got a spare
But I'd love it if you called me.

Hello Elena
I know, I know, I know
And sorry that I had to run away

It's shit – it is – it's really shit
Still I'd love it if you called me

FAZIL. So, um, so they're standing there
And I'm standing there
Just for half a moment, uh, until one –
'Fazil Mohammed?'

SHAYMA. **And I think it's important**
Really important we don't give up hope, y'know
And I know – I know it seems like –
I know it's slow
I know we'll get there in the end

FAZIL. Not like a question. Like a… um…
Statement. Accusation. Um. Sentence.
And I… No – I don't think I had the chance to answer.

KAYLEIGH. **And it's just that**
It's just that
That people move on

And you try to
Remind them
But people move on

Cos there's a lot going on and they get
They forget it's not over

FAZIL. Electoral roll, apparently – that was how they…
It's… If you don't opt out of the public one then…
Once they found the business they could
Um. Anyway. Never knew that.

SHAYMA. **Hi there Marianne**
It's Shayma calling you again
Um, Shayma – uh, from Filmore Kaufman Kane
I'll be in Kent again on the eighteenth
And I'd love to grab a coffee

KAYLEIGH. **So yeah we had our little setbacks**
Quite a lot of little setbacks
Cos it's a battle – a real battle, y'know

And you're fighting against apathy
You're battling that apathy
And if you don't –

KAYLEIGH *is interrupted by an (unheard) question.*

Who? Oh, the dentist. God.

FAZIL. And I know a lot of people think
People think dentists, y'know –
They deserve everything coming to them
Hah. But, but seriously…

KAYLEIGH. He – he, I mean – horrible, obviously –
The whole… But he was compensated for,
And he wasn't squeaky clean either.
He wasn't… The dentist isn't the story.
He was fine. Ultimately he was fine.

Now SHAYMA *picks up* KAYLEIGH's *chorus.*

SHAYMA. **And it's not that**
It's not that
That people don't care

No it's not that
It's not that
That people don't care

But there's a lot going on and it's tough
Can be tough so hang in there.

FAZIL. Anyway, I… Moved on? Maybe.
We did move. Um. Yes. Change of scene.
It was the door. Opening the door in the old place,
It became very, very difficult, um,
Especially if we weren't expecting anyone,
And that is… well, impractical.
Hah. For the place you live. So…
But we're settled now.

KAYLEIGH. **We call it empathy exhaustion**
Um yeah empathy exhaustion
Cos it's a battle – a real battle, y'know

And we all have our little setbacks
Sometimes quite a lot of setbacks
Too much happening – to keep track of it, y'know?

KAYLEIGH *goes*.

SHAYMA. **Sorry Benedict**
I just lost signal on my phone
I promise you I've not fallen behind
I know I ask a lot
But I'm really getting somewhere

And I think it's important
Really important we don't let them off, y'know?
And I know you have concerns –
But I am owed...
I know you'll thank me in the end

SHAYMA *hangs up and goes*.

FAZIL. Was that...? Is that everything you need?
Great. No, I'm fine. I...I do try not to, uh...
No I don't mind but, but I do hope that
Yeah. That I can let it die now.
No. No, not at all. Alright. Thank you.
And I can just...? Great. Okay. Great.

FAZIL *unclips his microphone and leaves*.

3. Zombie Hopkins

GRACE, *a journalist, emerges from the* COMPANY.

GRACE. Pick up your pitchforks – her posthumous popularity
is just another grizzly instalment of the Hopkins horror
franchise, writes Grace Harwood.

COMPANY. **359 comments**

COMPANY. **AlanIsAwesome commented on this
CorbynIsMyCopilot shared this**

GRACE. Like many, I long to bury Hopkins, but I refuse to
praise her.

COMPANY. **784 comments**

WEBSITE. This comment was removed by a moderator
because it didn't abide by our community standards.

GRACE. Ghoulish as it may sound, she would've been
delighted to die in the way that she lived – in a manner that
kept people talking.

COMPANY. **1041 comments**

WEBSITE. Replies may also be deleted. For more detail see
our Frequently Asked Questions.

GRACE. I fear the true tragedy may not be the loss of an
individual, but the immortalisation of her ideals.

COMPANY. **2328 comments**

WEBSITE. Comments will soon be closing on this article.
Thank you for your contributions.

Transition to a radio studio. JOEY, *a presenter, and* MARK,
his producer, are now talking to GRACE. *A jingle plays
them in.*

JINGLE. Big news, big views, no holds barred:
It's the water cooler with Joey King.

JOEY. Welcome back. Joining me now in the studio is Grace
Harwood. Grace is a journalist – a columnist for the
Guardian, that's right?

GRACE. Yeah. Well, not just… the *Guardian*, yes, amongst
    others –

JOEY. Sure.

GRACE. But not / in a –

MARK. Doesn't want you labelling her a *Guardian* writer.

GRACE. No –

JOEY. Ah – I see –

GRACE. No – not at all, / just –

JOEY. Grace would like to distance herself from the lentil-
    munchers, / but –

MARK. Ooh.

JOEY. Can I say that?

GRACE (*laughs*). You're… Okay, fine.

JOEY. Do you enjoy a good lentil?

GRACE. I… Sure. On occasion. Why not?

JOEY. Grace Harwood from the *Guardian* with her hot take on
    lentils, there. Now – seriously – seriously though, Grace is
    not – no one here is here to talk about… pulses? Mark –
    lentils – pulses?

MARK. Uh…

JOEY. I would ask Grace but I don't think she'd appreciate it.

MARK. Let's go with pulses.

JOEY. We're going with pulses. But – no, but Grace is here for
    – oh, okay, you'll like this – Grace has her finger on the
    pulse of another hot-button issue –

MARK. Nice. Almost worked.

JOEY. Almost, yeah. (*Laughs.*) We're here to talk about the late,
    great Katie Hopkins, aren't we, Grace?

GRACE. We are.

JOEY. You can't see this at home, but Grace did actually wince
    a little when I said 'great' just then –

GRACE. No, / that's –

JOEY. Little involuntary wince.

MARK. Little spasm.

JOEY. Tiny spasm. Because – fair to say – you're not her biggest fan, are you?

GRACE. That would be fair to say.

JOEY. Sure. Because this – I have here – this is the article you wrote to mark the, um, the six-month anniversary of her death. Here's the headline: 'Zombie Hopkins: The story that just won't die'.

GRACE. Yes. Now the / thing –

JOEY. And in it, you liken her to a – and I quote – 'a horror-movie monster who can never actually be killed off.' Zombie Hopkins – is that acceptable?

GRACE. I think… and for the record, just to – I do also at one point – I compare her to Jesus, um, rising from the dead, so –

JOEY. Just to make sure you've offended everyone.

GRACE (*laughs*). Ha. Yeah, to – yeah, we're very big on equal-opportunities offence at the *Guardian*.

MARK. Covering all the bases.

GRACE. That's right.

JOEY. But – okay, but in all seriousness – the language here – she's a monster, she's a zombie, she's spreading hate from beyond the grave – that's not –

GRACE. I… I think – the point / of it is –

JOEY. She's got kids – she's got a family out there.

GRACE. Yes, and that is obviously… Obviously that's… And what happened to her was – I'm not suggesting for a moment wasn't utterly despicable –

JOEY. But you think she deserves this?

GRACE. I think – yes! Yes, I… absolutely – one hundred per cent, / because –

JOEY. Really?

GRACE. Because listen – this is exactly the, the sort of fitting tribute she would… Yes, she's dead. Yes, she was killed in an awful, brutal, just absolutely… but – but look at her writing – her own / words – she was –

JOEY. Now hold on –

GRACE. She was the –

JOEY. You're saying she encouraged / whoever – ?

GRACE. No! No, no, not for a second. I'm just saying she was the least sentimental, the least mawkish, the least likely to be affected by… You know, the whole, the line – 'show me the bodies – I still don't care'. So, so / she –

JOEY. So you agree?

GRACE. I am saying it's a far more fitting tribute – far more in keeping – than this, this sanctification we're now seeing in some –

JOEY. So this is a tribute piece?

GRACE. No, but –

JOEY. Is 'zombie' a compliment nowadays?

MARK. Zombies are pretty trendy right now, / so –

JOEY. Trendy?

MARK. Sorry, is that not…? Zombies are 'on fleek' –

JOEY. Jesus.

GRACE. But look – listen – the point I'm making – the point of the article – is that we can't whitewash – we have to remember, in all of this all those things we found unacceptable, or, or offensive, or… That a tragic death doesn't alter what she stood for in life.

JOEY. And you think she'd agree with you on that?

GRACE. Honestly, I do.

JOEY. And do you think you've got a lot else in common?

GRACE. I, uh – (*Laughs*.) no, no I would think that's about it.

JOEY. But that is what we're talking about today – about legacy, about how we should remember – and you think we're getting this wrong?

GRACE. I think yeah. I think there's definitely been a, a rose-tinting, or even a hijacking in some instances, of... I think people are overlooking –

JOEY. So what do we need to know?

GRACE. Look, I'm not trying to prescribe a... Ultimately, I would love us to get to a point where we're not talking about her at all, actually.

JOEY. Right.

GRACE. Because / she isn't –

JOEY. And so that's why you've written this piece about her?

GRACE. I... No, that is... that was to challenge / the narrative of –

JOEY. Right. Well, you're going to stick around and take some calls, if you can bear it. How should we remember Katie Hopkins? That's our topic. Grace Harwood from the *Guardian* wishes she could be forgotten entirely, so that's why she's here live on the air with us. Who's on line one?

4. How Should We Remember?

It should feel as if the COMPANY *in this number are the various callers contacting the radio station – a mixture of grouped and single voices.*

JOEY. **How should we remember Katie Hopkins?**
MARK. **What did she stand for?**
JOEY. **What are you thinking?**

JOEY/MARK. **How do you remember Katie Hopkins?**
GRACE. **Pick up your pitchforks**
JOEY/MARK. **Keep people talking**

COMPANY. **And I think that as a mother**
　　And I think you can't forget the kids
　　And I think that as a business –
　　In a business sense she always did –

　　And I think that on the telly –
　　On the one with… What was that one called?
　　When she said that thing about them –
　　Though I don't agree with that at all

JOEY. **Do you still remember Katie Hopkins?**

COMPANY. **Yeah – and wi' kids, yeah**
　　Don't think it's fair to

JOEY. **Why should we remember Katie Hopkins?**
MARK. **What should it look like?**
JOEY. **Is this a tribute?**

Music shifts.

MARK. **Line One:**
COMPANY. 　　**Did the thing**
JOEY. **Line Two:**
COMPANY. 　　**Said the thing**
MARK. **Line Three:**
COMPANY. 　　**Controversial**

JOEY. **Line Four:**
COMPANY. 　　**On the show**
MARK. **Line Five:**
COMPANY. 　　**Got the sack**

JOEY. **Line Six:**
COMPANY.   **Had the comeback**

COMPANY. **A strong unapologetic woman**
And I know, well I'm sure, well I think she'd say –

A strong unapologetic woman
Who was bold, who was brave, well back in the day –

JOEY. **How should we remember Katie Hopkins?**
Do you remember?
Who thinks she stood for –

MARK. **Why should we remember Katie Hopkins?**
Try to remember
What seems important –

COMPANY. **How should we remember Katie?**

The COMPANY *go.*

5. One in a Million

SHAYMA *comes forward, making a presentation to a table full of her* CO-WORKERS. *Perhaps some sort of PowerPoint display accompanies her.*

SHAYMA.…That's all… You can hear me? Great.
Alright then. I know we're all busy so –
Thanks to Julie for Skyping in, hopefully that's all…
And Benedict, in particular, thank you for,
For this chance to… It has really…

So. McArthur Gledhill.
Twelve dead, including… including, uh,
Alek Nicolescu, who is the cousin of Elena
Who is a cleaner here, and just a…
Just an extraordinary person. So.

So. They aren't saying much,
But what they are saying is this was a,
A perfect storm – totally unpredictable –

Just a one-in-a-million confluence of events
That couldn't have been safeguarded against.
But, but okay, but let's look at those events.

To begin with it was freezing –
Below freezing that night – almost minus-two.
And, um, for any campers amongst you, you'll know –
Staying in a caravan when it's minus-two isn't…
And this was June, so they weren't prepared for it.
Those temperatures can threaten the whole harvest,
Even with, even in the polytunnels, a snap frost can…
So everyone's under pressure.
They have to scrabble around to bring in extra workers –
More than they'd been used to housing –
More than they could reasonably accommodate, I believe.

So it's minus-two.
And they provide these gas heaters. Calor gas.
Two were recovered, and McArthur Gledhill say
Only one of them was theirs – the other, it must've been –
One of the workers must have snuck it in, and,
And that's important,
Because the coroner did find signs of carbon-monoxide
poisoning,
Which could suggest a faulty unit, but what they're saying is
'That wasn't ours – it's not on us.'
And the, the poisoning – that would've been exacerbated
by…
They'd sealed the cabin up.
Any cracks – any ventilation – to try and keep the heat in –
So the fumes had nowhere to go
And again, McArthur Gledhill say 'look – they were told' –
'They sign terms of occupancy – they knew.'
And the source of the fire itself, it's inconclusive –
The investigators did find evidence of cigarettes
Which may or may not have been smoked within the caravans,
Which was forbidden, obviously,
But there's no proof that was how it started.

There's no proof they didn't supply the second heater, either,
And they can't explain why there were twelve people
In a unit meant for six – six at the most.

They claim they were just socialising there, but –
But I believe the bedding recovered suggests otherwise
And the cot bed – camp bed –
There was a camp bed that had to be dragged out
And pushed up against the door to use it,
To find space for it, so...
At least one of them was conscious –
Conscious at some point during the fire –
Because they were trying to get that door open
They could tell that from the positions of the bodies
But the bed, you see, it was lodged in the way –
It got stuck. You couldn't...

So if it hadn't been so cold
If they hadn't brought in the extra heater
If they hadn't sealed themselves in
If none of them smoked, maybe
If there weren't so many of them in there
If that camp bed hadn't got stuck...
Who knows?

These people were...
They weren't illegal. They weren't refugees.
They weren't hiding themselves in trucks
Or, or crossing oceans in leaky rowboats –
Not that – not that that would've been any better –
But these people, were... were just people.
Poor and foreign, and... and that was it
Just ordinary people
Trying to do their jobs
And they are entitled –

Y'know where was their march?
Where was their outrage?
Where was their viral campaign?
Their hashtag, their...?
Who had their backs?
It should be us. It should.
I believe that sincerely.

And I think we've a duty
We've a duty to do what we can, y'know?
And I know it won't be easy,

But even so
I think it might be up to us

I think we can help.
Filmore Kaufman Kane is in a position to help –
We can make sure they aren't forgotten.
So, who has any questions?

Lights down.

6. Special K

KAYLEIGH *comes forward. She speaks to us.*

KAYLEIGH. One – you've got to get people to care
    Two – you've got to find a way to keep their attention
    And three – three is actually making sure
    You can do something productive with it.

FRANKIE, *a vlogger, comes forward.*

FRANKIE. **Hello YouTube**
    Couldn't sleep last night
    Hello YouTube
    Had to get this out
    Had a little thought
    So please stick with me

KAYLEIGH. And a lot of the time, people were…
    Unfocused. Um. Not necessarily…
    Harmless mostly, but… Sorry –
    I'm trying to put this nicely…

FRANKIE. What can we – the online community –
    Do to make a real difference, yeah?
    I'm proposing a day for Katie.
    That's #Day4Katie –
    Let's really push this.
    Let's get this trending.

SHAYMA *returns, back on the phone. She's in a much better mood.*

SHAYMA. **Hi there Elena,**
We shouldn't get carried away
But yes I think it was a massive step
And now we've got some power on our side

Hi Beyoncé!
I think I've finally got some news
We're really getting somewhere with the case
And I'd love to fill you in

It shows it's important
It's so important we didn't give up hope, y'know
And I know – I know it has been –
It will be slow
But we will get there in the end

SHAYMA *leaves again.*

KAYLEIGH. But they weren't… It was meaningless
They weren't doing anything,
It was all just –

A number of VLOGGERS *enter, all making their videos.*

VLOGGERS. **Hello YouTube**
Here's what you can do
Hello YouTube
Time to show you care
Click the link to show
Your solidarity!

VLOGGER. Download your Katie Hopkins twibbon here –
Change your profile picture to –

STATUS. Katie Hopkins was brave enough to always speak
her mind.
Which of you will be brave enough to share this status
And let the world know that bravery still matters?

STATUS. Limited edition 'Special K' enamel pin badge
Commemorate #Day4Katie in style
With this exclusive design
Visit our Etsy page at –

KAYLEIGH. Cheap, ultimately. Cashing in, in this really
tawdry, um –

VLOGGERS. **How should we remember Katie Hopkins?**
Update your status
Download our twibbon

How should we remember Katie Hopkins?
Now we take PayPal
Won't be forgotten

Hello YouTube
Show you won't forget
Hello YouTube
Time to show you care
Like and share to show
Your solidarity!

KAYLEIGH. And opening themselves up for all sorts of –

STATUS. Some nutters online trying to organise a #Day4Katie
Why not make a donation to Refugee Action in her name
instead?

STATUS. To celebrate #Day4Katie The Fat Badger
Is offering two-for-one Katie-coladas.
Very strong and very sour, they're not to everyone's taste
But they sure pack a punch!

KAYLEIGH. Just childish. Just ludicrous.
And just when you thought it couldn't get any more –

FRANKIE *returns*.

FRANKIE. **Hello YouTube**
Let's not muck about
Hello YouTube
Getting real now
Check this message out
And then stand with me

Right. Okay. Here it is.
Because Katie – she made a real impact
And that demands a real, permanent tribute

*She rolls up her sleeve to show a large black 'K' tattooed on
her wrist.*

Here you go. My Special K.
Katie, you'll always be with us.

More COMPANY *members come forward, all with matching wrist tattoos.*

COMPANY. **A Special K for a special lady**
A Special K to show that you care
A Special K to pay tribute to her
A Special K that will always be there

KAYLEIGH. I mean Jesus. That anyone…
That after everything she could just end up as a meme –
As a joke, actually – as a dare –

More video footage. RYAN *is in a tattoo parlour filming himself on his phone.*

RYAN. Okay friends, so here I am –
A bet's a bet – no pussying out.
This one's for you Katie –
Get well soon!

Footage ends. RYAN *goes.*

KAYLEIGH. **I was sick of fakers**
All the losers and haters
And the ones who make out they really know her
But still no closer to –

COMPANY. **Justice, justice, justice for Katie!**

KAYLEIGH. **I was sick of coming up short**
And feeling like a failure
And being judged on their mad behaviour
And still no closer to –

COMPANY. **Justice, justice, justice for Katie!**

KAYLEIGH. **And I was tired –**
I was tired –
Of always being a punchline
Of always being sidelined
Of always losing the headline
To some bleach-blonde bimbo
With ninety thousand subscribers –
And that is tiring.

I was sick –
I was sick –

Yes I was sick and tired,
And tired of all of it
But I'm not a quitter
Cos she didn't quit
With all the shit that she got
I thought 'fuck it'
I'm sorry but 'fuck it'
Because she would never go out like this

I needed something lasting
I needed something legitimate
Because she was legit
And people don't see that
And then I had it
Suddenly just had it.

The voice of an official government WEBSITE *appears.*
This text could be spoken or somehow just projected/shown.
KAYLEIGH *sings over it.*

WEBSITE. One: You create a petition.

KAYLEIGH. **Something legitimate –**

WEBSITE. Two: You find five people to support it.

KAYLEIGH. **Something big – fucking big!**

WEBSITE. Three: We check your petition, then publish it.

KAYLEIGH. **Go big or go home. Go big like Katie did.**

WEBSITE. Four: The Petitions Committee reviews all petitions
we publish.

KAYLEIGH. **Something substantial. Something positive.**

WEBSITE. Five: At ten thousand signatures you get a response
from the government.

KAYLEIGH. **Something that she might be proud of.**
Something I could be proud of.

WEBSITE. Six: At one hundred thousand signatures your
petition will be considered for a debate in Parliament.

KAYLEIGH. **One:**
COMPANY.   **You create**
KAYLEIGH. **Two:**
COMPANY.   **Find support**
KAYLEIGH. **Three:**
COMPANY.   **We publish**

KAYLEIGH. **Four:**
COMPANY.   **We review**
KAYLEIGH. **Five:**
COMPANY.   **Government**
KAYLEIGH. **Six:**
COMPANY.   **They'll debate it**

KAYLEIGH/COMPANY. **A strong, unapologetic woman**
       Doesn't care – didn't care –
       Didn't wait to see

       A strong, unapologetic woman
       Who was shrewd – who was smart
       Undeniably

KAYLEIGH *now records her own video, with a link to her parliamentary petition.*

KAYLEIGH. **Hello friends**
       Thanks for tuning in
       Hello friends
       Here's what you can do
       Add your name below
       Make a real change.

7. Katie's Law

TV studio. A late-night news programme. KAYLEIGH *is being interviewed by* DOMINIC, *a straight-talking, somewhat superior journalist and presenter.*

DOMINIC. Joining me now, Kayleigh Harris, founder of the pressure group 'Justice 4 Katie' – Miss Harris, welcome.

KAYLEIGH. Thank you.

DOMINIC. And just so we're clear – Katie Hopkins is the Katie in question?

KAYLEIGH. That's right.

DOMINIC. And you don't believe she's getting justice already?

KAYLEIGH. No, I don't believe that. You only have to look / at how –

DOMINIC. But this is an ongoing investigation – the police / can't just magic up a –

KAYLEIGH. And I understand that, but / the truth of it –

DOMINIC. Resources are limited – she's not the only / unsolved –

KAYLEIGH. Of course not. But actually it's about more than… Justice in a very real sense, yes, but also about legacy.

DOMINIC. Indeed. Because tonight you're here to talk about your organisation's new initiative, and the petition you're hoping to bring to Parliament. This is 'Katie's Law'?

KAYLEIGH. It is.

DOMINIC. And the gist of this is – and do correct me if I'm wrong – but this petition would *repeal* – you want to get rid of our existing hate-speech legislation?

KAYLEIGH. We… We have a window, post-Brexit, to strip out a lot of unnecessary EU law, and within / that there's a –

DOMINIC. You want – hold on – so hate speech is a good thing?

KAYLEIGH. Free speech – free speech, Dominic. Justice 4 Katie / is –

DOMINIC (*with an amused smile*). Forgive me for sounding blunt, but have you gone completely insane?

KAYLEIGH. If you'll allow / me to –

DOMINIC. Last year you were working in the charity sector – now you want to start tearing up the Human Rights Act?

KAYLEIGH. Well look – listen – the Human Rights Act is fundamentally, is pretty flawed and redundant, actually, in lots of… but it doesn't have / anything to do with –

DOMINIC. I'm sure there are many millions who / would –

KAYLEIGH. But I'm… But it's not about that. I'm talking about our own actually insane legislation, dressed up in the most misleading language that makes us… So let's get this straight – I'm not saying I'm all for hate speech – I'm saying I'm for free speech, and hate speech doesn't exist.

DOMINIC. It doesn't?

KAYLEIGH. It does not.

DOMINIC. Really?

KAYLEIGH. People use 'hate speech' nowadays to mean any opinion they don't agree with. Well grow up – it's sticks and stones, Dominic – even children know this – sticks and stones may break my bones but words can never hurt me.

DOMINIC. But words can / be used to –

KAYLEIGH. No – it's a nonsense. And we can't make laws against calling people names – that is an abuse – that is dangerous.

DOMINIC. Dangerous how?

KAYLEIGH. By, by – just look! By getting people killed!

DOMINIC. How has – ?

KAYLEIGH. By criminalising opinion. By labelling those with controversial opinions criminals – hatemongers – monsters – you legitimise them as targets. You say 'oh, she had it coming' – you are blaming – you are trying to blame women for their own murders – you / are endorsing a –

DOMINIC. But no one – no one has seriously suggested –

KAYLEIGH. They have! Of course they have! Everywhere you look in this liberal, all-welcoming utopia we are being taught that it's more of a crime for a woman to speak her mind than it is to murder that woman in cold blood! This / is the –

DOMINIC. Now come / on, there has been –

KAYLEIGH. Open – open your eyes, Dominic! Look! Everyone knows this. We saw… We watched a prominent British figure gunned down in our capital city, and twenty-four hours later we saw celebrations, people who came to, to celebrate in the streets, just like – like the Muslim – the Arab countries after 9/11, taking / pleasure in the death of –

DOMINIC. Hold on – now just hold on, you're not suggesting –

KAYLEIGH. Of – of one of our own – of a / respected –

DOMINIC. But those people weren't… They weren't foreigners or Muslims, were they? / They were British –

KAYLEIGH. I believe some were, but…

DOMINIC. We're talking a handful of people / in, in Glasgow, and…

KAYLEIGH. People gloating – people / taking pleasure in –

DOMINIC. And people who would – under your proposal – get off scot-free?

KAYLEIGH. No. Not free from criticism. And we already have plenty of laws for public conduct, uh, violence, vandalism, destruction of property – actual crimes –

DOMINIC. Alright, okay, but I guess what I'm… In this day and age, with all the anger, the violence, the bloodshed on our streets – how can you look at that and say 'yes, a little bit more hate is just what we need'?

KAYLEIGH. Because we do! A little bit of hate is… There's nothing wrong with that – not when you're at war. You say 'hate', I say passion. I say it is justified, it is right – to hate some things – to hate violence and hypocrisy and yes – and the influx of, of radical foreign ideologies who hate women

and freedom and act in the most repellent, oppressive... I am
proud to hate them. I hate the erosion of our communities
and jobs and values and being told that we are to blame – not
the Government, not the terrorists, not the media elite, but *us*
– we're garbage, we're terrible, we should be ashamed of
ourselves. Enough! It is a national joke, and I don't find it
funny any more.

DOMINIC. And this is... A lot of your rhetoric would certainly
seem to echo Katie Hopkins' own. But you weren't always a
fan, were you?

KAYLEIGH. I... I wasn't... I think like a lot of people I didn't
always / appreciate how –

DOMINIC. 'How can anyone defend her? How do you even
start to say something nice about someone so toxic?'

KAYLEIGH. Okay, so let's just... It's that kind of ignorance
that I / really –

DOMINIC. Those were your words – written the morning after
her death, in fact – in an internal email to one of your then-
colleagues –

KAYLEIGH. I... Let me... I wasn't...

DOMINIC. You went on to call her 'poisonous', 'hateful',
'someone / who – '

KAYLEIGH. Okay, okay, that's... So this is... clearly this is an
ambush, a / hijacking, but –

DOMINIC. 'No one should want any association with, alive
or dead.'

KAYLEIGH. And I... as I said, I didn't initially, I / admit –

DOMINIC. And this is a – I'm told this is a vomiting emoji,
you sent / to –

KAYLEIGH. Right. Yes. I wasn't... But also, let me be clear –
this isn't really about Katie Hopkins. The / whole –

DOMINIC. It isn't?

KAYLEIGH. No. This / goes far beyond –

DOMINIC. Justice 4 Katie isn't about Katie Hopkins?

KAYLEIGH. I... obviously / there's –

DOMINIC. Katie's Law isn't about Katie Hopkins?

KAYLEIGH. Listen, Dominic, you can bully me all you like. I shan't be intimidated.

DOMINIC. I'm only quoting / your own –

KAYLEIGH. I know what I believe in. I'm not ashamed of it.

DOMINIC. Very well. One final question: 'crackpots, Nazis and the mentally ill', that's how you described Ms Hopkins' supporters at the time. Do you feel at home amongst them now?

KAYLEIGH. I... I don't recall ever... They are, uh, very fine people, and I am proud to represent them.

DOMINIC. And that's all we have time for. Kayleigh Harris, thank you for joining us.

8. Have You Seen This? (Part 1)

Music plays. The COMPANY *come forward as various online commenters, talking about the interview we've just seen.*

COMPANY. **Have you seen this?**
Were you watching this last night?

Have you seen this?
Swear this woman's proper crazy!

Have you seen this?
Right-wing scum is getting owned!

Have you seen this?
Look at her, she's full-on Nazi!

BRANDON *updates his status.*

BRANDON. Dearly beloved – please stop sending me the link to that video. Kayleigh and I are not – I repeat, ARE NOT dating any more. Seriously – your guesses regarding her mental state are as good as mine!

UPDATE. **Jessica West and thirty-nine others like this**
Crying with laughter!
Crying with laughter!
Crying with laughter!

COMPANY. **Disgusting**
This woman's totally disgusting
I can't believe that people can be
It makes me sick right to my stomach

Disgraceful
I think she's totally disgraceful
I hope she's properly embarrassed
She makes me sorry to be British

Is she taking the piss?
This woman
Has it now come to this?
This woman
Christ what have we started?

Have you seen this clip yet?
This woman
You'll love this one, I bet
This woman
Christ what have we started?

COMMENT. Typical lame-stream media stitch-up, just like they tried on KH – good on you Kayleigh.

COMPANY. **A hero!**
I think this woman is a hero
At least she's trying to be honest
She's saying what we all are thinking

Disgusting!
The way she's treated is disgusting
He's such a patronising arsehole!
I can't believe I even watched this!

And we always defend –
Always quick to defend
To forgive to excuse
Y'know foreigners
All the immigrants
And the benefits – the claimants

9. Allahu Akbar, Motherfucker

A Tube carriage. SHAYMA (*wearing a headscarf*) *sits.* MAN 1
is standing, swaying slightly, in front of her. He is well-spoken,
wears a smart suit and appears drunk. He is filming her on his
phone, and we also see this footage projected live. Other
members of the COMPANY *present as other commuters.*

MAN 1 (*to* SHAYMA). Say something then. Go on. Say
something to the boys and girls at home.

SHAYMA *angles herself away from him.*

What? What's the matter? Hello? Can you hear me?

MAN 2. Here, mate, come on –

MAN 1 (*ignoring this*). Do you speak English? English?
Parlez-vous Anglais? (*Giggles.*) Are you allowed to speak?

MAN 2. Knock it off –

MAN 1. You're not, are you? Back home they're not… not
allowed out of the house without a, a man, a minder.

MAN 2. Mate –

MAN 1. Who's minding you?

MAN 2. Mate, can / you just – ?

MAN 1 (*now turning around*). Look, just fuck – fuck off, I'm
not your mate, so –

MAN 2. Take it / easy.

MAN 1. I'm having a conversation. I'm allowed to do that. We are still allowed to… She isn't, obviously, but in this country – in this / country, right –

SHAYMA. Can you stop filming me please?

MAN 1. She speaks! She can! It's a miracle!

WOMAN. Leave her alone.

MAN 1. Does no one else…? I'm trying to get to the bottom of… I'm doing you all a public service. She's probably… Y'know they send the – their women and children, all wired up, all… (*Back to* SHAYMA.) What's in your bag?

SHAYMA *gets up and tries to move away. He blocks her path.*

Hey! Hey! Not so fast –

SHAYMA. Excuse me please.

MAN 1. Where do you think you're going?

SHAYMA. Home.

MAN 1. Oh, *home*. Great. No, that's… When's your flight then? Home! When are you going to fuck off out of here?

MAN 2 *now tries to get between them.*

MAN 2. That's enough / now. Just –

MAN 1. I have warned / you not to –

MAN 2. You've had a bit much. You're / making a –

MAN 1. Back off – just back off mate, alright? I saw her first, so… Fucking White-Knighting all over… No. (*Back to* SHAYMA.) How much though? Go on – I mean it – how much?

SHAYMA. Don't touch me.

MAN 1. I'm joking! Jesus – it's a fucking… You think I'd touch you? You couldn't pay me, love. Fucking hell. Don't… Don't you look down your nose at me. Your days are numbered. We're coming for you. We're waking up. We're done with… just you wait. You'll come begging, on – on your hands and knees – for a big strong man like me. So what d'you say?

Lights suddenly shift. All apart from SHAYMA *are frozen,
as we cut to an interview. She sings to us.*

SHAYMA. **He wasn't a partner**
But he was probably going to be a partner
If not there then somewhere
A going-places person, y'know

And he could be quite charming
Not quite as charming as he thought he was
Um, and not unattractive
In a sort of unimaginative way

And he wasn't a monster
These people aren't monsters
These people are people
And that's the real problem
Because monsters are easy

And there are rules of course about workplace…
And I don't think I encouraged –
Thought it was friendly,
A bit flirty
But basically fine
Until it wasn't fine…

And he closes the door
And he won't let me leave
And he's standing too close
And his hand's on my knee
And it isn't fine
Right then it isn't fine

And he wasn't a monster
They don't have to be monsters
They're really just people
And that's the real problem
Because monsters are easy

And you are praised for slaying monsters
People are grateful.
People weren't grateful.
People were angry
Because they liked him

And he did good things
And he wasn't a monster

But they don't have to be monsters
They don't start out as monsters

I am done, I am done with –
I don't take that now
I am a dragon-slayer
I'm not frightened of monsters –

Song ends. SHAYMA *takes her place again and the scene unfreezes.*

SHAYMA (*rummaging in her handbag while talking*). What've I got to say?

MAN 1. Yeah. Speak up for... What're / you – ?

SHAYMA. Uh-huh? Allahu Akbar, motherfucker.

On this line, SHAYMA *has removed a small canister of pepper spray from her handbag, which she sprays into* MAN 1's *face. He screams and the phone is dropped to the floor. Immediately other* COMMUTERS *are on their feet trying to separate them. General commotion, panic, shouting.*

MAN 1. Ah! Fuck! Fucking bitch! What did I...? Jesus!

The projected image freezes.

10. Have You Seen This? (Part 2)

COMPANY. **And we always defend –**
   Always quick to defend
   To forgive to excuse
   Y'know foreigners
   All the immigrants
   And the benefits – the claimants

*This next exchange is the transcript of an online forum. We
perhaps see the text scrolling as well as hear it. We might
also see the CCTV footage of the tube carriage being shared.*

Have you seen this?
Muslim psycho on the Tube

Have you watched it?
Anyone seen this reported?

Don't believe this!
Just look what we're coming to

Send a message!
Share and get the cunt deported

Disgraceful!
I swear this girl's fucking disgraceful!
Isn't this just what I was saying?
Bet they don't put this in the papers!

Disgusting!
That man is totally disgusting!
I pray to God that he's arrested!
I'm sick to death of this whole country!

I'd love to get my hands on them
I'd love to – just five minutes yeah
Five minutes yeah and lock the door
I'd show you something special

Allahu Akbar motherfucker!
Allahu Akbar motherfucker!
Allahu Akbar motherfucker!

As the song ends, a still from the CCTV footage lingers.
COMPANY *goes.*

11. Colossal Lady Balls

A late-night comedy show. The host, behind a desk, is STUART. *To his side, two guests,* TERRY *and* PIPPA.

STUART. Well, that is one badass Jihadi mother–[*bleeped*].

Studio laughter.

I mean it. How cool is she? Now – okay, look – now I'm not condoning this entirely. I would like to say that violence isn't always the answer, but *come on*. She is – Pippa, am I right?

PIPPA. Oh yeah. Amazing. She's like a, a feminist Islamic Arnold Schwarzenegger.

TERRY. I think you've just described most of Stu's sexual fantasies.

STUART. Yeah, it's a – no, it's a niche set of filters on Pornhub, I'll admit that.

PIPPA. Jesus.

STUART. Damn right though. I love her. I do. Come on – who's not a little turned on watching that? Who doesn't have a big old boner for aggressive multiculturalism? It's nothing to be ashamed of.

TERRY. You've plenty to be ashamed of.

STUART. Shut your face. So, so this woman, she's been identified – her name is Shayma Hussaini. She is – British citizen, not that it matters – smart woman – trainee human-rights lawyer – one of the good guys, no question. And / she has –

PIPPA. Has she got into trouble for this?

STUART. She – so she's been let off with a caution for now. Been getting – getting a lot of stick online – lot of the usual –

TERRY. And it is a bit... I don't know, not to be... But I mean for a lawyer, it's not the smartest... 'Yes, m'lud, in my defence I would say I was shouting "Allahu Akbar" ironically – '

More laughter.

STUART. Alright, sure, but even so – the balls on her, right?

PIPPA. Colossal lady-balls, absolutely.

TERRY. That's your, um, that's your superhero name, isn't it?

PIPPA. Captain Colossal Lady Balls. Uh-huh.

STUART (*through laughter*). Okay, okay, but, but no, I think she's a hero – genuine hero. I do. I think – alright, this is the point: Yes, she escalated, and, and just thank God we're not in America and this cock-weasel wasn't armed, but ultimately she stood up for herself, she refused to play the victim, and she kicked some ass. So, Shayma Hussaini – I might rather have you in my corner in a street-fight than a murder trial, but nonetheless I salute you. You are Late Night Fight's Inappropriate Role Model of the week.

A jingle plays.

BAND. '**Inappropriate Role Model of the Week!**'

STUART. Lovely stuff. Brilliant. Now moving on. Moving on, it's time to name our Weekly Wanker –

BAND. '**Late Night Fight's Weekly Wanker
Late Night Fight's Weekly Wanker
Wanker of the Week!**'

TERRY. Late Night Fight's Weekly Wanker is brought to you by Kleenex tissues: Kleenex, the wanker's choice.

STUART. Stop it – stop saying that – it's not – you're going to get us sued.

More laughter.

Right. Okay, right – now, Pippa, as our guest of honour we asked you to pick our wanker this week. So who did you come up with?

PIPPA. Yes. Lots of tempting options. Spoilt for choice, really, but I've gone for a somewhat lesser-known wanker, I think, and that is Kayleigh Harris.

TERRY. Who?

PIPPA. Exactly.

TERRY. Is this just someone you went to school with? Because that's a pretty... impressively petty, but –

STUART. No, this is – I know this person – I did recognise her when I looked her up – she, she has this organisation – 'Justice 4 Katie' –

PIPPA. Yep.

TERRY. Katie who?

STUART. That would be Katie Hopkins.

TERRY. Oh Jesus.

STUART (*laughing*). Yeah. I know, but... Anyway, she's got this petition going, and she did an interview last week with... Well, let's just have a look –

A clip from KAYLEIGH*'s interview plays.*

KAYLEIGH. A little bit of hate is... There's nothing wrong with that – not when you're at war. You say 'hate', I say passion. I say it is justified, it is right – to hate some things – to hate violence and hypocrisy and yes – and the influx of, of radical foreign ideologies who hate women and freedom and act in the most repellent, oppressive... I am proud to hate them.

Clip ends.

STUART. And that's quite enough of that.

TERRY. Just a spoonful of hatred helps society collapse –

STUART. Okay. Okay, so Pip – this petition she's started – do you want to give us the gist of it?

PIPPA. Sure. So she's basically – and it's pretty bold – but essentially she's saying what the world needs now is more hate speech.

TERRY. Uh –

STUART. Right. So it's... It's basically the whole 'free speech' argument, isn't it?

PIPPA. Yeah, in a 'let's put *Mein Kampf* on the National Curriculum' sort of way.

TERRY. Well I think she sounds lovely.

STUART. No, I mean she is batshit, undeniably, but, but we also found this – you're going to love it – just take a look. Roll the clip.

Another 'clip' plays, and/or is performed live. This is an auto-tuned remix of the interview.

REMIX. **Okay**
Let's get this straight

There's nothing wrong with
A little bit of hate

Justice 4 Katie is
Flawed and redundant

It's that kind of ignorance
I want to celebrate

You say 'hate' – I say passion
Hate! Passion!
Hate! Passion!

You say Katie I say repellent
Katie! Repellent!
Katie! Repellent!

I'm all for hate
I'm all for hate

Clip ends – back to the studio.

PIPPA (*wiping away a tear of laughter*). Oh God, that's incredible.

TERRY. Oh, you beautiful internet weirdos with far too much time on your hands –

STUART. Be nice. I think that's genius. Okay Pippa – take us home.

PIPPA. Right, yes, absolutely. Gather round children. Listen carefully. This is how the world ends – by being too idiotic to call idiots idiots. By being so obsessed with the idea of everyone's opinion being valid that we hear lunatics calling for a race war and rather than calling the police we book them in for *Newsnight*. Fuck this woman. Fuck her and everything she stands for.

TERRY. Don't hold back there, Pip.

PIPPA. Oh, I won't. And this idiot wasn't even always an idiot. No – she was a charity worker – she was a humanitarian – and now... So I'm sorry, she needs to be an example – she needs to be a laughing stock – we can't let her live this down. This is what happens when they get to you. What is it they say? 'Lie down with dogs, and you're going to get fleas.'

TERRY. That's the classiest way I've ever heard someone get called a bitch.

STUART. Absolutely – we're all about the class here. Alright. So, Kayleigh 'Hate Speech' Harris, you are our weekly wanker, and to sing us out with a little ditty in your honour – it's Ollie the work-experience boy, everybody!

OLLIE, late teens, enters. He's dressed in drag, in a crude and glammed-up version of KAYLEIGH's *interview outfit. It should be clear who he's meant to look like.*

TERRY. That poor boy.

STUART. He loves it really. Now remember, these are all the exact words you said, Miss Harris – we might've just had a little fun with the order of them. Thanks to my guests, Pippa Goldstein and Terry Drake, thank you all for watching, and we'll see you next week. Goodnight.

OLLIE and the BAND *perform a lounge/swing version of the remixed song. It could be a bit of a budget production number, with 'Katie' cancan girls, etc. We might also see the footage from the original interview played behind them, cut to fit.*

OLLIE. **Okay**
Let's get this straight

There's nothing wrong with
A little bit of hate

Justice 4 Katie is
Flawed and redundant

It's that kind of ignorance
I want to celebrate

You say 'hate' – I say passion
Hate! Passion!
Hate! Passion!

You say Katie I say repellent
Katie! Repellent!
Katie! Repellent!

I'm all for hate
I'm all for hate
I'm all for hate
I'm all for hate

We're garbage – we're terrible – everybody knows
Justice 4 Katie is a national joke
Criminals – hatemongers – monsters
I want an all-welcoming Utopia for those

Open your eyes!
I am to blame

Justice 4 Katie is
Actually insane

I don't believe
In human rights

I believe in
Calling people names
We should be ashamed!

We're garbage – we're terrible – everybody knows
Justice 4 Katie is a national joke
Criminals – hatemongers – monsters
I want an all-welcoming Utopia for those

You say 'hate' – I say passion
Hate! Passion!
Hate! Passion!

You say Katie I say repellent
Katie! Repellent!
Katie! Repellent!

You say 'hate' – I say passion
Hate! Passion!
Hate! Passion!

You say Katie I say repellent
Katie! Repellent!
Katie! Repellent!

I'm all for hate
I'm all for hate
I'm all for hate
I'm all for hate
I'm all for hate
I'm all for hate
I'm all for hate
I'm all for hate!

Scene ends.

12. An Example

The COMPANY *come together – sharing clips of* KAYLEIGH*'s humiliation.*

COMPANY. **Have you seen this?**
　　Jesus Christ the fucking state!

　　Were you watching?
　　What a classic bit of telly!

　　Can't believe this!
　　How can that girl show her face?

　　What a takedown!
　　Proper classic bit of telly!

We now see KAYLEIGH *and* SHAYMA *caught up in the middle of it all, trying to hold it together, making calls, sending messages, etc.*

COMPANY. **Have you seen this?**
SHAYMA. **Yes I know it isn't great**

COMPANY. **Do you know her?**
KAYLEIGH. **No, I swear I'd no idea**

COMPANY. **Can't believe this!**
SHAYMA. **Please just tell me what to do**

COMPANY. **That'll show her!**
KAYLEIGH. **Shit – I think there's someone here**

> *The* COMPANY *surge forward, now sharing both*
> KAYLEIGH *and* SHAYMA*'s personal details. The CCTV*
> *footage of* SHAYMA *is still being shared too.*

COMPANY. **That's her profile**
Isn't that her sister?
This is who she's working for
Get the message out there!

Found her! Found her!
Got her! Found her!
Flat 6b, Newlands Close

Found her! Found her!
Scare her! Rape her!
At Filmore Kaufman Kane

> KAYLEIGH *and* SHAYMA *sing together.*

KAYLEIGH. **And we all have our little setbacks**
SHAYMA. **And I don't think he's a monster**
KAYLEIGH. **Quite a lot of little setbacks**
SHAYMA. **Cos I don't believe in monsters**
KAYLEIGH. **Cos it's a battle, a real battle y'know?**

SHAYMA. **I don't think, I don't think**
That people are bad
No it isn't as simple
As 'people are bad'
But we get carried away
And we get, we forget to be human

KAYLEIGH. **And it's difficult to blame them**
SHAYMA.   **But I do believe in people**
KAYLEIGH. **It really does no good to blame them**
SHAYMA.   **I think I still believe in people**
KAYLEIGH. **It's just human nature y'know**

SHAYMA *goes*.

COMPANY. **I'd love to get my hands on her**
KAYLEIGH.   **Something legitimate**
COMPANY. **I'd love to just a little chat**
KAYLEIGH.   **Something that she might be proud of**
COMPANY. **I'd love to she deserves a taste**
KAYLEIGH.   **Something I could be proud of**
COMPANY. **We'll make her an example!**

KAYLEIGH.   **And I almost had it**
              For a moment I had it
              I thought that I'd found it

KAYLEIGH *prepares a statement*.

Dear Friends,
It is with great sadness that I am resigning with immediate
effect as Chief Executive and spokeswoman for Justice 4
Katie. While I remain utterly committed to our cause,
I believe that my continued involvement is no longer in the
organisation's best interest. I would like to apologise
unreservedly to anyone who has been upset or felt let down
by my actions, and I hope that others will fight on to achieve
the successes I was unable to.
Wishing you courage and good fortune.
Yours,
Kayleigh Harris.

She goes.

COMPANY. **Amazing!**
This show is totally amazing!
I don't know where they find these people
But still it's bloody entertaining

The COMPANY *go*.

13. Your Official Update

SHAYMA *enters. She has a laptop and a water bottle. She is clearly very drunk. As she turns on her webcam, her face is projected across the stage.*

SHAYMA. Hello. Hellooo world.
Hello tiny people inside the internet.
Greetings.

She swigs from the bottle.

This is – don't worry, this is water –
Staying hydrated – very important.
Stay hydrated kids. Anyway.
This – this is your official update
From Filmore Kaufman Kane!
Because no one else
Nobody in this company understands social media
(*Sing-song.*) and I have all the passwords.
Yes. I do.
They took my keycard but I can still –
I have the power. Yes.
And with great power comes great
Comes a great social responsibility to…

So I was fired today. Yeah.
Big day. Big day for me.
Big, um, big uptick in Twitter followers
But also very fired so
So swings and merry-go-rounds
Not merry-go-rounds
Swings and… whatever
I was fired. I was 'let go'.
I have proven myself to be a liability
And it's… it's hard to argue with that really.
I am a mouthy brown lady and that
That is frowned upon, so
I'm not – for the record –
I'm not saying *they're* racist
I'm saying – what I'm saying is –
I was racially abused
By someone entirely else

And then I was fired for it, so
So go figure – you go draw your own…

It's fine.
I have a bright future ahead of me.
Very bright. I'm very bright.
No, I am, I promise
You don't… Don't you worry about me
Worry instead about the… the…
Because they are fucked now – that's the real…
Because nobody else gives a shit –
Nobody even knows their names, so
So okay. Let's do this, as the least I can…
It's bad luck to toast with water,
But at this point, to be honest, fuck it. Alright.

She sips. As she names the dead, she drinks to each of them.

Alek Nicolescu.
Andre. Andre Dalca.
Aris Spiros.
Camille Dobrescu
And Mada – not Mada –
Reka Dobrescu. Sisters.
Mada Cutov.
Donna and Lexi Zlatkov.
Cousins.
Um. Alek, Andre, Aris.
Camille and Reka.
Donna and Lexi.
Mada. I said Mada.
Nicole… Moisil.
Peter Draganov.
One before Victor. Sara.
Sara Balan and Victor Groza.
That's the twelve. And. Phew.

And you don't know who they are
Nobody knows who they are
Nobody cares. So. Yeah.
Look 'em up. See if
See if you can be more helpful than I was.
Here's to them. Anyway.

Cheers. And sorry. And
Let this bear witness
Stand testament for all of time
Until they figure out how to reset the accounts
And. And yeah.
This is Shayma Hussaini
Signing off for Fuckface Kaufman Cocks
Take it easy guys.
Night night.

She leans forward and turns off the camera.

Alek. Andre. Aris.
Camille and Reka.
Donna and Lexi
Mada, Nicole, Peter
Sara Balan, Victor Groza

And you don't know who they are
Nobody knows who they are
Nobody cares. So.
Look 'em up. See if you…
Here's to them. Anyway.

Now KAYLEIGH *returns. Their songs overlap.*

KAYLEIGH. **One: Powerful**
SHAYMA.   **Alek, Andre, Aris.**
KAYLEIGH. **Two: Honesty**
SHAYMA.   **Camille and Reka.**
KAYEIGH. **Three: Hard-working**
SHAYMA.   **Donna and Lexi.**

KAYLEIGH. **Four: is clever**
SHAYMA.   **Mada. Nicole. Peter.**
KAYLEIGH. **Five: is funny**
SHAYMA.   **Sara Balan**
KAYLEIGH. **Six: not a victim**
SHAYMA.   **Victor Groza**

KAYLEIGH. **A strong unapologetic woman –**
SHAYMA.   **And you don't know who they are**
KAYLEIGH. **Doesn't care – didn't care –**
SHAYMA.   **Nobody knows who they are**

KAYLEIGH. **Didn't wait to see**
SHAYMA.   **Nobody cares, so**
KAYLEIGH. **A strong unapologetic woman**
SHAYMA.   **Look 'em up**
KAYLEIGH. **Who was shrewd – who was smart**
SHAYMA.   **See if you**
KAYLEIGH. **Undeniably**
SHAYMA.   **Here's to them. Anyway.**

They sing together.

KAYLEIGH/SHAYMA. **We call it empathy exhaustion**
    Um, yeah, empathy exhaustion
    Cos it's a battle, a real battle y'know

    And you're fighting against apathy
    Worse than anger is the apathy
    Too much happening to keep track of it, y'know

    And it's not that,
    And it's not that
    That people don't care

    I don't think it's
    As simple as
    People don't care

    But there's a lot going on, and it's tough,
    Can be tough so hang in there.

    And a lot can go wrong, and it's tough
    It's enough to hang in there.

They go.

14. Our Own Little Bubbles

A few snippets from news bulletins.

JOURNO 1. A damning new report on the future of the NHS. New / figures show –

JOURNO 2. Could Harry and Meghan soon be expecting twins? Our psychic predicts double trouble may soon / be on the way.

JOURNO 3. Red faces for the Justice 4 Katie movement – a march expected to attract thousands brought fewer than two dozen attendees to Birmingham.

We now gradually move into the characters from 'Where Were You When?' First up, PAM, RICHARD *and* NINA.

PAM. And it was – who was it?

RICHARD. Cynthia.

PAM. No, it wasn't Cynthia. She was –

RICHARD. Wine-club Cynthia.

PAM. Oh yes. Yes, that Cynthia. Our friend Cynthia, and she said –

NINA. We use her as a case study now. In, um, in Media Studies – persuasive writing – she's one of our –

RICHARD. She'd thought that –

PAM. I'm telling it.

NINA. It's her, Charles Dickens and Joseph Goebbels, so…

RICHARD. Sorry.

NINA. Quite the, um, prestigious…

PAM. So she'd – yes – so she'd… We were talking about, about Katie, and the protests, and it turned out all this time / she'd –

RICHARD. She'd been thinking of –

PAM. Shh. But yes, she'd been thinking of, oh, what is her…? Who was married to –

RICHARD. Tom Cruise.

PAM. Cruise! Yes. Katie Holmes – that's who she was picturing, every time, and I was just...

RICHARD. Some people.

PAM. Staggered, that some people, yes, can be so... So out of touch.

COMPANY. **How should we remember Katie Hopkins?**
Should be respectful
Um but remember

How should we remember Katie Hopkins?
Um but remember
Uh what she stood for

How should we remember Katie Hopkins?
How do you start to?
Why would you want to?

How should we remember Katie Hopkins?
What did she stand for?
Why should we bother?

Now SHAYMA *and* KARL *have also joined in.*

NINA. And Charles Dickens – Dickens is interesting actually, because we think of him as... But he, um, he wanted to talk about the poor laws, about cruelty to children, Government corruption –

KARL. It was mental.

NINA. Things nobody else is –

KARL. And it was mental how mental it got, looking back at it.

SHAYMA. I'm sorry, what's this for?

NINA. So he gets on stage, and he courts controversy, and he says some shocking, some awful things about –

KARL. Proper crazy. I'd forgotten, actually.

SHAYMA. I don't – it's not that I mind, I just don't really understand why you're asking me about her.

NINA. About um Jewish people for instance – truly horrendous – but he stoked up fury and provoked conversation and that conversation provoked real change. So… I'm not saying she's Dickens – or Goebbels, but… What am I saying?

COMPANY. **And I think that as a mother**
And I think that's easy to forget

And I think that as a fighter
And she seemed to live with no regrets

And it's hard to remember
And I think a lot got misconstrued

And I think that now it's over
There's a lot of thinking still to do

BRIAN *and* OWEN *have now joined.*

SHAYMA. I'm not trying to be awkward.

BRIAN. But I do think – I will say this –

KARL. It's funny, y'know?

BRIAN. Some of the, um, of the people who emerged in the aftermath – who it brought out of the woodwork, well –

OWEN. I had a row with one of my producers once because I wanted to put the Westboro Baptist Church on the telly –

BRIAN. They weren't the sort of –

OWEN. Cos they were over doing a tour, and I thought… but my producer, one of my producers was dead against it uh 'you can't have these people on, they're mad'.

SHAYMA. I'd just rather –

OWEN. And I'm like 'put them on, cos if you expose, if you give them the rope to hang themselves with just like otherwise people don't hear the utter insanity of it, and you get this filtered, this corrupted or watered down' –

BRIAN. Do we want to give those kind of people a voice? Honestly?

OWEN. Because you can't silence… People, those kind of people, they're going to go online and find out whatever anyway so I say just get it all out there.

COMPANY. **And I think a sense of humour**
And I think she always spoke her mind

And I think that there was anger
But it does no good to be unkind

Still it's hard to remember
What she stood for – fought for – I recall

But I think that you should leave her
If you've nothing nice to say at all

Now KAYLEIGH *has joined the group. One by one, having spoken, the others will draw back, leaving her by herself.*

KAYLEIGH. We all live in our own little bubbles. I was in my own lovely little left-wing bubble where we were all happy and nice we're all nice to each other and enraged by the same things and we don't –

RICHARD. But I think ultimately –

PAM. I say rest in peace – I say draw a line and –

RICHARD. And there's an end to it.

KAYLEIGH. We don't realise the strength of feeling that comes from other places.

NINA. So that is a, uh, a legacy of sorts, I suppose.

KAYLEIGH. We don't listen.

KARL (*chuckles*). Like a dream, almost.

KAYLEIGH. We don't hear any voices other than our own, and that, that is…

OWEN. And I don't think – no – I don't think it's actually going to make anyone support the Westboro Baptist Church. No.

KAYLEIGH. Dangerous. Actually dangerous.

BRIAN. I think the less said about her now the better.

KAYLEIGH. And those voices, they have to be big and brash and extreme – to cut through –

SHAYMA. Are we done? Thank you.

KAYLEIGH. But without a voice you're nothing.

COMPANY. **How should we remember Katie Hopkins?**
Try to be kind, but
No sugar-coating

Why should we remember Katie Hopkins?
None of this spiteful –
None of this gloating –

How can we remember Katie Hopkins?
Who really knew her?
Who can be certain?

Who thinks they remember Katie Hopkins?
Who has a picture?
Who knew the person?

KAYLEIGH. Katie Hopkins is free speech. Like it or not, she is the entry point into the argument and from there you find your own way, but without her... It takes someone special, someone Teflon, and I realised... That wasn't me. Because there was a moment, a moment after my, uh, my own little public shaming, when I could've really doubled down, leant into it, embraced that whole kind of unapologetic public enemy sort of, of... and I was tempted, and in some ways it was probably the closest, actually, I ever got to properly understanding her, a little glimpse of what it must've been like to... And I couldn't. I didn't want it. Because what must it do to you? (*Beat*.) Anyway. No, no regrets. That's another philosophy: no regrets allowed. YOLO. Do you remember when we used to say YOLO? (*Laughs*.) Right. Great. Is that everything?

KAYLEIGH *starts removing her microphone as others come forward as* JOURNALISTS.

JOURNO 1. Amongst the losers in last night's local elections, Kayleigh Harris. The former charity worker and founder of the ill-fated Justice 4 Katie movement failed to / gain a –

JOURNO 2. Another farcical setback for the England football team, sent crashing / out of –

JOURNO 3. An investigation into the deaths of twelve fruit-pickers in Kent has found no evidence of wrongdoing. Justice Peters said while this was an unspeakable tragedy, there / was no –

JOURNO 4. In other news, the Metropolitan Police issued a statement today saying they were suspending their investigation into the murder of media personality Katie Hopkins. Hopkins' death sparked public outcry and even mass demonstrations last year, but a spokesperson said there was no new evidence with which to continue their inquiries. Now we go to Tina with the weather.

JOURNALISTS *go.* KAYLEIGH *has now finished taking off her microphone. She passes* SHAYMA *entering. They recognise each other but don't speak.* KAYLEIGH *leaves.*

15. British Justice

A press conference. SHAYMA *stands centrally.* ELENA *to one side,* CATALINA *to the other. Various* JOURNALISTS *watch them.*

ELENA. Good afternoon, my name is Elena Nicolescu.

CATALINA. Hello, I am Catalina Cotrus.

SHAYMA. And I am Shayma Hussaini –
    You might remember me from such viral sensations
    As 'Muslim psycho on the Tube'
    And 'Drunk intern slams bosses'.
    Um. Best to get that out of the way with.
    Not my finest hours. Ahem. Anyway.
    We are here today to officially launch British Justice,
    A new not-for-profit organisation.
    British Justice might not be what you think it is
    But it means exactly what it sounds like.

Making sure the British justice system works
For anyone who finds themselves here,
Be they foreign nationals, refugees,
Asylum-seekers or native citizens,
That our British values of democracy,
Of tolerance, acceptance and compassion
Are upheld and extended to all.

We have a proud justice system –
One of the best in the world
And it's there for everyone
That's the reason it exists
But not everyone knows about it
Not everyone understands it
But the whole point of it being there
Is to protect those people –
The most vulnerable –
To ensure justice isn't reserved
For the wealthy, for the privileged,
For the ones who know how it works.

Justice shouldn't be selective
It shouldn't be able to be bought or sold
Or based on what you know or who you know
That's the idea, anyway
And that's the idea of us.
To provide / justice –

She is interrupted by a bleeping message.

COMPANY. **Have you seen this?**

SHAYMA. To provide justice – to be a voice for the voiceless –

More bleeps and messages. One by one the JOURNALISTS
start to go to their phones, singing their messages.

COMPANY. **Have you seen this?**
Don't believe a word of it.

SHAYMA. Providing free legal counsel –
Counsel to those who don't realise they're entitled to it –

COMPANY. **Have you seen this?**
Urgent

Have you seen this?
Urgent breaking
Have you seen this?

SHAYMA. We're here because we believe justice shouldn't
come with a price tag, that –

Now she's totally lost them.

COMPANY. **We're getting news that there has been**
There has been some / kind of
Kind of emerging –
Some urgent –
Emergency –

Have you seen this?
Someone / get on this right now
Get on this before we lose this story

Have you seen this?
Swear to / God you won't believe it
God you won't believe these people!

Have you seen this?
It's / the one we're waiting for
The one that everybody's dreading

Have you seen this?

Drop it and call me – call me now!
Stop what you're doing!

Have you seen this?
Have you seen this?
Have you seen this?
Have you seen?
Have you seen?!

End.

www.nickhernbooks.co.uk

 facebook.com/nickhernbooks

 twitter.com/nickhernbooks